ENDORSEMENTS

"For some years I have enjoye[...] Now I'm delighted to see him in p[...] ten and well-informed. He writes [...] two most important contexts of Phil[...] ...ginal setting in the ancient world and the setting of our lives today or "what it meant to them" and "what it means to us." I learned quite a bit about both from reading Dan's book along with Paul's letter. I recommend Dan's commentary to anyone who wants to learn more about Paul's gospel—and that should be everyone."

– Dr. John Frame
Professor of Systematic Theology and Philosophy Emeritus
Reformed Theological Seminary

"Dan Lacich takes us on a journey through Paul's mission to the church in Philippi, taking in the historic and geographical setting and unpacking Paul's own missionary ambitions as we go. As we walk through the text of Philippians, we are given a sense that we are making the missionary journey along with Paul; and thus, can easily cross the centuries and cultures to our own mission today. We come away freshly invigorated to do as Paul did: hopeful and expectant that we will have courage to exalt Christ by both our life and our death (Philippians 1:20), and eager to live Christ-formed lives that are worthy of the gospel (Philippians 1:27; 2:5)."

– Rev. Dr. Simon Vibert
Vicar of Christ Church Virginia Water
Virginia Water, England

PROVOCATIVE
JOY

Living Well,
No Matter What

Dan Lacich

HigherLife Development Services, Inc.
P.O. Box 623307
Oviedo, Florida 32762
(407) 563-4806
www.ahigherlife.com

Printed in Canada

10 9 8 7 6 5 4 3 2 1

Joy fills Paul's letter to the Philippians.

My life is filled with joy because of the forty-plus years I have been honored to call Barbara Maguire Lacich my wife.

This work is dedicated to her, and would not have been possible without her encouragement, counsel, wisdom, and love.

TABLE OF CONTENTS

FOREWORD

Provocative it is not a word usually associated with how we think Christians are supposed to live. Most of the time it conjures up visions of outrageous behavior exhibited by the dress or behavior of a super model, celebrity, or even a politician. We expect *provocative* behavior on the fashion runway, red carpet, or the evening news. Most Christians take pains to avoid being provocative, especially in dress, speech, and everyday conduct. However, there is a very real sense in which Christians not only can, but *should*, be provocative!

In my first book, *Provocative God: Radical Things God Has Said and Done*, I dealt with passages in the Bible that *should provoke* some kind of response from of us. Yet for one reason or another—either because they are so challenging that we ignore them or so familiar that they have become powerless clichés—these passages no longer provoke a reaction. For instance, when God commands us to love our enemies that should provoke some kind of response. We should be bewildered over how to do that, pushing back and saying that's impossible, or considering the idea with deep introspection in our heart of hearts, asking God to change us. What is not possible nor acceptable is to glibly quote those verses and move on.

In a very real sense, God is a provocative God. *He intends to provoke a response from us.* When He made the provocative demand on Abraham to offer up Isaac as a sacrifice, He expected a response from Abraham. When He confronted Moses through the burning bush that was not consumed, He was provoking Moses to action. When Jesus called Peter, Andrew, James, and John to drop their nets and follow Him, He was provoking them on several levels. First of all, it was unusual for a rabbi to seek out followers in this manner. It was just not the way things were done! Normally, the follower picked the rabbi. Second, calling them to leave their families was a radical step in such a family-oriented culture. Finally, telling them that they were going to change their careers and place in society by following Him was really beyond the pale. Clearly God does things to provoke a response.

But it is not only God who is provocative. Followers of Christ are expected to be provocative as well. My life verse is found in 1 Peter:

But in your hearts honor Christ the Lord as holy, always being prepared to make a defense to anyone who asks you for a reason for the hope that is in you; yet do it with gentleness and respect. *(1 Peter 3:15)*

While that verse is a favorite among those of us who love apologetics (the science of defending the faith), there is something much deeper here. There's a reason we should always be ready to defend our faith. It's because people have seen something different in us and have asked about it! In this case Peter says this will happen when they see your "hope" and wonder where it came from! We are to be ready to point to Jesus. In other words, when your hope (your life in Christ) provokes a question (when it is *provocative*), you have opened the door to proclaim the gospel that you have been demonstrating.

Not only can our hope be provocative, but as seen clearly in Philippians, our joy is provocative. Much like Martin Luther King Jr. writing *Letters from a Birmingham Jail*, Paul is writing letters from a prison; and this particular letter to the church in Philippi is a letter filled with joy. More than a dozen times, in a very short space, Paul speaks of his joy or that of the Philippians. What makes this all the more provocative is that Paul is awaiting a trail that could result in his execution. Joy in the midst of such life-and-death circumstances cannot be ignored. It forces the question: "How did he not only speak of joy, but actually remain joyful in such circumstances?" The answer for Paul always goes back to Jesus and the gospel.

While the scantily clad model is trying to be provocative in a lustfully enticing sense, Christians are to be provocative in a *spiritually* enticing sense. Our love for God and our neighbor should draw people in, and cause them to ask why we are like that. Where the politician or even the revolutionary calling for change is trying to stir people to action, the follower of Christ is doing that too: calling people to action and seeking to provoke a response for Jesus.

This book then is also seeking to be provocative. It is a commentary, or explanation, of Paul's letter that will hopefully help you become more like Jesus. Each chapter is divided into two parts: What This Meant to Them and What It Means to Us. The first is an explanation of what Paul's words meant to his original hearers, the Christians in the young church at Philippi. In their cultural context, they would have instinctively understood much of what Paul was saying. They would have seen quick connections to their situation in the words, illustrations, and nuances of Paul's letter. In order for us to understand how it applies to us today, we need to understand what it meant to its original audience. Like all of God's Word, it was written for us, but it was first written *to them*, the original audience.

The second half of each chapter digs into the message and its implications for us today. While there are certainly many similarities between first century Roman culture and ours, there are also very clear differences. My hope is that you will grow through digging into Philippians and this book; and as a result, be able to apply God's truth to your life better than before. When that happens, you may just find yourself living a *provocative Christian life* that others want to know about.

– Dan Lacich

ACKNOWLEDGEMENTS

Any work of creativity is never the result of the efforts of one person. This book is no exception. There are numerous people who deserve recognition and my thanks. There are too many to mention them all, yet some must be acknowledged.

I am grateful to the elders of Oviedo City Church who have supported and encouraged me in my teaching and writing in general, and this book in particular. Fred Franz, Doug Hill, Peter Katauskas, Eric Linares, John Nasby, and Dave Welday, working alongside you is an honor, as we fulfill the mission of "Being Disciples Who Make Disciples."

The staff at Oviedo City Church is the best team I could ever hope to work with. Our regular staff Bible study in which we have dug into Philippians has added to my understanding and appreciation of Paul's letter. Brian, Bre, Kortnie, Kelly, John, Lauren, Kristen, Jaci, April, and Joy, you have my undying thanks. I look forward to every day that I get to spend serving Jesus alongside you all. Special thanks to Brian Katauskas, the Executive Pastor at OCC. His feedback and encouragement on the earliest draft was the kind of motivation I needed to press ahead. Without his leadership gifts in our church, I would not have had the bandwidth to finish.

On Tuesday nights, for the last three years, Barbara and I have hosted an Oviedo City Small Group in our home. It is a college and young adult group, except for the two of us. Deep thanks to the group who spent months, studying and applying Philippians together and helping me see even more applications. This process made me able to write a better book than I would have without them. Not only have they added to this book, but they have all added to my growth in Christ in different ways. Seabass, Lakelyn, Lauren, Justin, Kendall, Eric, Brandon, Olivia, Jordan, Katie Leigh, Jared, Erik, Brandy, Bernie, and Gabby, thank you!

The team at Higher Life Publishing has done the unbelievable in getting this book in print so quickly and so well. Thanks to Dave Welday and Nicole Fraser for directing the project and fast tracking it so it can be available in time for a church-wide study at Oviedo City Church. I am especially grateful to Ellen King for the wonderful job of editing. Not only did she complete the time-consuming job of correcting punctuation and spelling, but more importantly, made it a much more compelling and readable book.

INTRODUCTION
DO NOT SKIP THIS! THE CHURCH IS BORN!

It was not part of the strategic plan. Paul had no intention of going to Philippi in Macedonia to preach the gospel or plant a church. No. Paul's original plan was to take the gospel further into Asia, to the area we commonly call Asia Minor, which is today the western portion of modern Turkey. However, in one of the more startling passages in the Bible we are told this:

> And they went through the region of Phrygia and Galatia, having been forbidden by the Holy Spirit to speak the word in Asia. (Acts 16:6)

Paul and Silas had left Antioch and traveled cross-country to Galatia where Paul and Barnabas had previously preached the gospel and planted churches. From there they continued deeper into that territory, planning to preach the gospel. It was a reasonable plan. They had taken the gospel so far and intended to extend it to the next territory adjacent Galatia and Phrygia, but through means the Bible does not explain in detail, they become convinced that the Holy Spirit was forbidding them from preaching in that area. They didn't simply say that the door was closed to them, or that people failed to respond. Somehow the Holy Spirit had made it clear that they were not allowed to preach the gospel there.

Imagine what it must have been like for them! Having laid out this great and perfectly reasonable plan to take the gospel to people who had never heard it before and doing all they could to fulfill Jesus' command to preach the gospel to all nations (Matthew 28:18-20), the Holy Spirit forbid them from going! Somewhere in there is a lesson about God's ways not being our ways. What seems logical and reasonable to us is not always what God has in mind.

> ## What seems logical and reasonable to us is not always what God has in mind.

So what did Paul, Silas, and Timothy, their young disciple, do? Well, they prayed and made another plan, just as we would do. They determined that the next best option was to go north through Mysia and then east towards Bithynia.

There was a whole wide open field for ministry in that part of the world, but their plans were thwarted by God once again.

And when they had come up to Mysia, they attempted to go into Bithynia, but the Spirit of Jesus did not allow them. (Acts 16:7)

Two attempts to preach the gospel; two rejections by God. Now what would you do? For Paul and his group the answer was to head west towards the coast on the Aegean Sea and then turn south, taking the gospel to the cities there. Surely this must be where God wanted them to preach because they were seemingly out of options, or so they thought. What never crossed their minds was the possibility of heading west *across the Aegean Sea!* That, however, was exactly what God had in mind.

During the night as they slept in the coastal town of Troas, Paul had a dream that he was certain was the work of God. In his dream he saw a man of Macedonia beckoning him to come over and help them (Acts 16:9). Finally Paul had a direction that he knew would not be thwarted by God, but was God's desire and plan. So off they went. Traveling north by ship along the coast, they arrived in Macedonia at Samothrace and then the harbor town of Neopolis. From there they traveled a short distance inland to the key city of Philippi.

Philippi was a city with a unique history that had a major impact on the founding and ongoing life of the church there. Originally named for Philip of Macedon, the father of Alexander the Great, it eventually became a key Roman colony filled with Roman citizens, many of whom were retired military. It was a Roman city on Greek soil.

In March of 44 BC, Julius Caesar was assassinated by a group of Roman senators on the steps of the Roman Senate. Among the conspirators were Gaius Cassius and Marcus Brutus of Shakespeare's *"Et tu, Brute!"* fame. Seeking to avenge the assassination of Caesar, Mark Antony and Octavian formed a coalition and declared war on Cassius and Brutus. They fought a decisive battle near Philippi in 42 BC with Mark Antony and Octavian victorious, and Brutus and Cassius committing suicide in defeat. As a reward to their veteran soldiers, Mark Antony and Octavian declared Philippi to be a Roman colony and provided land for their retiring veterans to settle in that area.

Being both a Roman colony and a retirement center for Roman soldiers gave the area a decidedly Roman culture, a sense of patriotism, and strong Roman pride that were not found in many places outside the city of Rome itself. You can easily compare it to places like Norfolk,

Virginia or Fayetteville, North Carolina in the United States, places with large military bases and large populations of retired veterans and their families. There is a distinct culture, a pride of accomplishment, a sense of duty, and a loyalty to country in these areas, that is more intense, evident, and deeply held than you will find in an average American town.

That was certainly the case in Philippi. The city was filled with Roman soldiers and their descendants. They were the bad boys on the block who had conquered most of the known world. They were proud to be Roman citizens and soldiers. They were the men who kept order in a chaotic world, something Rome highly valued. They were a cut above everyone else. They were also loyal to Caesar to the point of carrying out the regular ritual of making sacrificial offerings to him as though he were a god, yet another practice the Romans had picked up from their Greek forebears. The inhabitants of Philippi may have been living in Macedonia in the midst of Greek culture, but they were thoroughly Roman, practicing Roman law, promoting Roman values, and exhibiting Roman dominance.

As Roman citizens they had rights that the average person did not. Among those was the right to appeal to Caesar if a court case went against you. Citizenship also meant that you were exempt from certain punishments. This became important when the city leaders discovered that they have beaten and imprisoned Paul, a Roman citizen, without the benefit of a trial. The average person could be treated that way, but not a Roman citizen. Citizens had rank and rank had its privileges.

ARRIVAL IN PHILIPPI

When Paul and his companions, Silas, Luke, Timothy and possibly a few others, arrived in Philippi, they spent a few days getting acquainted with the city. When the Sabbath arrived, they began to look for some Jews to begin sharing the message of Jesus the Messiah. Heading outside the city gates, they looked for a place of prayer where they expected the small Jewish population of the city to have gathered (Acts 16:11-13).

It has been common for people to assume that because Luke used the phrase "place of prayer" in Acts 16:13, and that this place was outside the city, near the river, that the Jewish community in Philippi did not have a building and were meeting outdoors. Although that is one option, some recent scholarship indicates that it is far more likely that they actually did have a synagogue in which to meet. While Luke does not use the Greek word for synagogue, *sunagoge,* he does use the word *prosuexe* or place of prayer. This word is often translated as "synagogue" when referring to a Jewish place of prayer. "The fact that the place of prayer was outside the city walls does not preclude that they were meeting in a building. Some diaspora Jewish communities preferred to build their meeting places outside the city near a body of water. The river could be used for ceremonial immersion" (Schnabel2012, 679). The fact that Paul and his companions walked to the river because they assumed that it was where they would find the place of prayer makes sense, if it was a common practice to put a synagogue there as Schnabel states.

As idyllic and inspiring as it may sound that this group of people were meeting for prayer outside next to the river because they were not allowed to build a synagogue in the city, it is far more likely that they met in some sort of synagogue near the river by choice. As a *religio licita* or "approved religion" under Roman rule, the Jewish community in Philippi would have been permitted to build a synagogue within the city. They could also just have easily met for prayer in any of their homes without fear of persecution or retribution.

What is more uncertain is why Paul and the group speak only with the women who had gathered. Many have taken this to indicate that there were no men present and that as a result there was no synagogue (because they did not meet the Jewish rule that required the *presence of ten men* to form a synagogue). There are however other possible reasons for this. Perhaps the men were unwilling to speak with Paul and his companions; it is even more likely that the men and women prayed separately and at different times. Paul and company may have simply arrived at a time when only the women were present.

Whatever the circumstances, present with that group of women was Lydia, a woman of some means, who ran a business selling purple cloth. She was intrigued by the message and came to faith along with her entire household. They got baptized and became the core of the first church in Philippi, which was the first church in Europe proper.

Things quickly took a bad turn in Philippi. When Paul was on his way to the place of prayer, he picked up something of a stalker. Luke tells us that a young girl who was demon-possessed began to follow them around for several days, declaring the following:

"These men are servants of the Most High God, who proclaim to you the way of salvation." (Acts 16:17)

Eventually, Paul was fed up with this unwelcome testimony and finally cast the demon out of the girl. The trouble began when her masters, who used her as a way to scam money out of people, discovered that their source of income was no longer available to them. They brought charges against Paul, and he and Silas were beaten and tossed into prison for disturbing the peace and promoting customs that were strange, foreign, and presumably damaging to the Roman culture of Philippi.

It all seems rather swift and arbitrary when we read that they were beaten and tossed into prison so quickly, but consider two factors: First, there was a Roman obsession with keeping order in Philippi. Paul and Silas were clearly in the middle of some kind of disturbance of the peace. Second, they were the outsiders here, the unknown party. The charlatans who made money off the demon-possessed girl were known residents of the city, and probably had some wealth and standing. It was their word against two strangers and the accusations could not have been more damning:

"These men are Jews, and they are disturbing our city. They advocate customs that are not lawful for us as Romans to accept or practice." (Acts 16:20b-21)

Beaten and imprisoned, Paul and Silas decided that having a little worship service was the right thing to do. They spent the night in jail singing praises to God and in all likelihood telling anyone within earshot of the wonderful good news of Jesus. When an earthquake broke open the jail, the Philippian jailer assumed his prisoners had all fled, so he prepared to take his own life, knowing that it was forfeit anyway because of his failure to do his duty and keep the prisoners from escaping. Suddenly the voice of Paul cried out from the darkness, urging him not to harm himself for they were all still in the jail.

Three things took place at this time that are of utmost importance: The jailer came to faith in Christ. He took Paul and Silas to his home to care for them where his entire household, meaning blood relatives, servants, and anyone else who looked to him as the *pater familias,* or family patriarch, also became part of the newly formed church of Philippi. Finally, the jailer learned that Paul was a Roman citizen who has been *unlawfully* beaten and tossed in jail!

When the magistrates learned of this the next day, they were in a panic. Now *they* (and not Paul) had broken the Roman law. Unlike today where a series of lawsuits would surely be in the works, Paul asked only for an apology. Upon receiving it and having a chance to speak to the brothers and sisters of the newly formed church, Paul and friends headed out to take the gospel to other parts of Greece.

Estimates for the timing of Paul's first visit to Philippi range between AD 49 and AD 52. Some scholars are confident in the AD 49 date (Fee1995, 27), while others prefer the range between AD 49 and AD 52 (O'Brien1991, 5). For our purposes, the exact date is not important. If we work with an approximate date of AD 50, and accept that Paul was writing while he was imprisoned in Rome and awaiting his appeal before Caesar, then we have about a dozen years between the founding of the church and this letter.

It must be acknowledged that Rome is not universally accepted as the place of origin for the writing of Philippians. Some scholars have suggested that it may have been written from Paul's imprisonment in Caesarea prior to getting to Rome, but Paul's time in Caesarea would not have had the life and death tension that this letter contains. The reason this tension was not evident in Caesarea was mostly due to the fact that Paul still had the appeal to Caesar in his back pocket, so to speak. If the happenings in Caesarea became as life-and-death as the letter to the Philippians suggest, then Paul would have simply appealed to Caesar and put off an impending execution. Ephesus is also suggested as the place of his imprisonment and the writing of this letter, since it is closer to Philippi and would have allowed the back-and-forth visits of Epaphroditus and others that are mentioned in the letter. The problem is that we have no evidence of Paul ever having being imprisoned in Ephesus. All in all, the traditional view of Rome as the city of origin still best fits all the evidence.

THE YEARS IN-BETWEEN

Paul continued his relationship with the brothers and sisters in Philippi after he and Silas left the city. In fact, the Philippian church became possibly his most ardent and faithful supporters over the next dozen or so years. Not only did they support him financially in the ministry, but also labored alongside him, staying in close contact with him. They prayed for, and in some respects, shared even in his sufferings as he took the gospel to the world. He expressed his gratitude for that relationship in the beginning and the end of his letter to them. (See Philippians 1:5 and 4:15-16.)

In the dozen or so years between the founding of the church and the writing of the letter from a prison in Rome, Paul had taken the gospel to Thessalonica, Berea, Athens, Corinth, back to Ephesus, and once again to Philippi and many other Greek towns and villages on a return trip through parts of Asia Minor and Greece. After all that, he ended up back in Jerusalem again. According to Acts 21, in Jerusalem, Paul was arrested and eventually sent to Rome for his appeal to be heard by Caesar. All along the way, the Philippian church was near and dear to Paul's heart.

The relationship is so special that unlike many of his letters in which Paul is defending his ministry or adamantly opposing some aberration or distortion of the gospel, the letter to the Philippians is filled with affection and love. There is an openness and warmth that permeates this letter. It follows much of the ancient pattern of a friendship letter, which included certain protocols of greeting: reminiscence of the relationship, thanks for support, and updates of the current state of affairs (Fee1995).

For roughly four years leading up to the writing of this letter, Paul had been a prisoner for the sake of the gospel. This began with his arrest in Jerusalem where it took better than two years to bring some sort of movement in his case. The trip to Rome was as dramatic as they come with a shipwreck along the way (Acts 27:13-44). By the time Paul reached Rome, he was put under house arrest with a small contingent of Roman soldiers guarding him day and night. It also appeared likely that one of those soldiers would have been chained to Paul at all times (Schnabel2012, 1066).

JOY, JOY, JOY!

One theme stands out in the four chapters of Philippians: *joy*. This is true for two reasons. The first is the simple fact that Paul mentions "joy" or "rejoicing" more than a dozen times. This short letter is completely saturated with joy and rejoicing! That's why the chapter titles of this book all have the word "joy" in them, and why the title itself is about joy.

The second reason that joy is so central to the work is the context in which Paul was writing. It is startling that Paul speaks so often of joy and rejoicing at the very time he is awaiting word on whether he will be set free by Caesar or quite possibly have his head separated from his body as a death sentence. That was exactly what would happen if Paul was found guilty of disturbing the peace of the Roman Empire and leading people into rebellion by urging that they follow a king other than Caesar. It is shocking and bewildering to read this letter in that context. From his imprisonment as he was waiting to hear his fate, Paul was filled with joy and urging others to be filled with joy and rejoicing too. That is not the typical attitude one would expect from a person peering over the abyss at their impending doom. Yet here is Paul filled with *real joy!* He is not delusional or putting on a good show for the Philippians to keep their spirits up. He is genuinely rejoicing in the Lord and wants others to do the same.

More will be said about joy and rejoicing as we deal with the particular passages in which it is found. However, some groundwork must be laid first. The biblical concept of joy, at least as Paul makes use of it so often in Philippians, has little or nothing to do with one's immediate circumstances in life. It is not the equivalent of feeling happy. It is not some charged-up version of happiness on steroids. Happiness is all about what is happening. It is about the happenstances of life. If they are going well, then one should be happy. If things go badly, then being unhappy is understandable and expected. Paul's circumstances would easily have justified his being unhappy, but that didn't seem to cross Paul's mind. His circumstances (the happenstances of his situation) were irrelevant to his outlook. He had something deeper than conditional happiness. He had real joy in the Lord, which trumped everything that was going on, even the possibility of his own beheading.

Joy is about one's relationship with the Lord—regardless of the circumstances. We find our joy in the Lord, in our relationship with Christ and the salvation that relationship brings. Paul often wrote about being "in Christ." It is *in Christ*—in a relationship of trust and faith in Christ, in which we find our ultimate joy because we have found our ultimate purpose and fulfillment and are assured of our ultimate end. If your salvation is secure in Christ, knowing that "he who began a good work in you will bring it to completion at the day of Jesus Christ" (Philippians 1:6), then all the happenstances of life are minor by comparison. If you know Christ and are assured of being found *in Him* on the day of judgment, then indeed rejoice! So whether one will be set free or executed by the judgment of Caesar, one can still rejoice in Christ.

CHAPTER 1

THE JOY OF GRACE AND PEACE

¹ Paul and Timothy, servants of Christ Jesus, to all the saints in Christ Jesus who are at Philippi, with the overseers and deacons: ² Grace to you and peace from God our Father and the Lord Jesus Christ. (Philippians 1:1-2)

WHAT THIS MEANT TO THEM

The Christians in Philippi would have been introduced to this letter when Epaphroditus brought it to them on his return from ministering to Paul on their behalf. The letter would have been read publicly before the entire church. Given the tender relationship between the brothers and sisters in Philippi and the apostle Paul, it is safe to say that they listened with great anticipation. They wanted to know how Paul was doing, what the latest news was regarding his imprisonment, whether or not Paul thought he would be set free soon, and the progress he had made in preaching in other parts of the empire.

Paul's opening greeting, the opposite of standard letters today, begins with introducing himself and those with him—in this case, Timothy. Of course they would already have known that the letter was from Paul, but nevertheless he started with an introduction rather than a "to whom it may concern" opening, and waiting to the end to sign off as Paul.

Although he mentions Timothy, this is really a letter from Paul. "Paul is the sole author of the letter...Timothy is probably mentioned because he had played such an important role in the preaching of the Gospel (sic) in Macedonia and Achaia (Acts 16-18). He had ministered faithfully during Paul's imprisonment, and the Philippians had a special attachment to him (2:20-22)" (O'Brien1991, 44). The letter comes from their father in the faith directly to them, his children and partners in the gospel.

Paul described himself and Timothy with a provocative term. The ESV translates it as *servants* of Christ Jesus. However, the Greek word Paul used was *douloi,* the plural of *doulos.* In the Philippian world, this meant *slaves.* They heard Paul and Timothy call themselves *slaves* of Christ. Slaves were common in the Roman world; and while they did not generally suffer the kind of torment associated with slavery in the Antebellum South of the United States, they were still slaves, bound to the will (and whims) of a master. Given the Roman pride in the population of Philippi, the idea of being a slave would have been repugnant to most of them. Yet at the same time, it is reasonable to assume that there were slaves within the church. There could even have been slaves within the households of some of the more wealthy Christians. It is not out of the realm of possibility that Lydia and others had slaves in their households who were also brothers and sisters in Christ. Slavery was common in the ancient world.

Given that both slave and free would have been listening to this letter from Paul, there must have been diverse internal reactions to Paul's self-designation of *doulos*. The slaves within the church would have surely heard a note of solidarity. Here was Paul, their spiritual father, identifying himself as a slave—just like them. Granted he was a slave to Christ and not to a human master, *but he was a slave nevertheless*. For a person bound in slavery, this had to have been a greeting that lifted their hearts. To know that Paul identified with them and also saw himself as a person under a Master, granted a sense of dignity and hope to any slaves in the congregation.

Those who owned slaves may very well have been surprised by this greeting. Paul, calling himself a slave, probably seemed odd, even inappropriate, to many of them. In a Roman world that idolized power, identifying as a slave was as countercultural as one could get.

What is of interest at this point is what Paul does *not* say. It was normal for him in his letters to churches to address his readers and remind them of his position as an apostle. (He did this in Romans 1:1; 1 Corinthians 1:1; 2 Corinthians 1:1; Galatians 1:1; Ephesians 1:1; and Colossians 1:1!) Only here in Philippians and in his letter to the Thessalonians, another Macedonian church, did Paul *not* refer to himself by his office as an apostle.

There are a few reasons why this is the case. Often in his other letters to churches Paul was in a position in which he had to assert or reassert, as with the Galatians and Corinthians, his position as an apostle. This was often due to serious internal strife in those congregations and major moves away from the heart of the gospel that Paul had preached among them. There was no such need with the Philippians. Their affection for Paul and his for them is obvious and strong. He didn't need to remind them of his apostolic authority.

He can come to them in the humility of a slave and in the bonds of affection made strong over years of mutual service to one another.

When Paul addressed the Philippian church, he spoke of three different groups. First there were the *saints in Christ Jesus*. The saints, *hagiois,* are those who had been set apart. This is the root word for "holy." The saints are *the holy ones in Christ*. This was not a subset within the church of Philippi, but referred to *all* who were in Christ, *all* who had a saving trust in Christ and were thus set apart in Christ: the slave, the master, the businesswoman, the jailer, the retired Roman soldier, the pimple-faced teenager, the city official, the farmer—they were all one people now. They would have heard in the use of the word *hagiois* that no matter what their various differences in the world were, they were all united and had a common identity. It is reminiscent of Paul's words to the Corinthians that they were all one body.

> **Being set apart is at the heart of what "holy" means in the Bible.**

For in one Spirit we were all baptized into one body—Jews or Greeks, slaves or free—and all were made to drink of one Spirit. (1 Corinthians 12:13)

Not only would being saints (or holy ones) reinforce their sense of oneness in Christ, it would also have told them that they were set apart. Being set apart is at the heart of what "holy" means in the Bible. Things that were considered holy were things set apart for God's use and purpose. The holy objects in the temple: the bowls, altar, incense stand, and all the rest were holy—not because of some intrinsic value or purity of their own, but because they were set apart to serve God for a purpose. To be called *saints* by Paul was to be reminded that God had set them apart for service too. They were a people belonging to God, in much the same way that Paul and Timothy where *doulio,* slaves set apart for a purpose by God.

Living in the midst of a Roman colony in which countless people saw themselves as special, set apart, a cut above the common folk, it was a startling statement to tell people they were *set apart by God Himself.* They were special, a cut above. The average Roman citizen would have taken great pride in being set apart as a citizen. It would have been an honor passed down from generation to generation, as was the case with Paul's citizenship. Or it would have been purchased at a steep price requiring much sacrifice, or even conferred for invaluable service to the empire. In any case, citizenship was a badge of honor and pride because it marked that person as set apart from the crowd as a citizen of the great Roman Empire.

Paul is taking this idea to another level, explaining what it means to be a citizen of heaven. This citizenship, however, was not something that had been passed from an earlier generation. They were the first! Additionally, this citizenship was not something they could purchase. Nor could they earn it. It was a gift. But oh, such a gift that it was an honor to be set apart for service to the True King. Serving Caesar and being set apart in service to the empire was one thing, but serving King Jesus and being set apart in the service of His kingdom was far greater. All of the followers of Christ in Philippi heard that they, saints that they were, had been set apart by God for the highest of honors—to be called His and serve Him.

Paul also addressed two subgroups within the church: overseers and deacons.

Overseer comes from the word *epsicopos* from which we get the word "episcopal." It is sometimes translated as "bishop" in English. Overseer was a common enough term and referred to people who had some responsibility to keep watch over a country or a people. (O'Brien1991, 47). In the case of New Testament churches, the overseers would have been those people given charge to guard the flock, protecting it from heresy and harm.

The deacons were the third group mentioned in Paul's greeting. Their role would have been more directly involved in serving the needs of the flock from a practical and pastoral perspective. The Greek word *diakonos* is often transliterated as deacons. The Philippians would have understood this to mean servants or ministers.

Everyone in the church was a saint, a holy one, set apart by God for His purpose. Overseers had the added responsibility of making sure the saints were protected, taught, and led well. The deacons had the responsibility of serving the practical needs of the flock. By greeting the whole church and these various groups, Paul was getting everyone's attention, making sure they knew this letter was specifically for them. Paul was also reinforcing the responsibility that the overseers and deacons had by mentioning them. What he was about to write to the whole church applied especially to those in leadership.

Now that Paul had the attention of everyone in the church, he pronounced a blessing: *Grace and peace to you from God our Father and the Lord Jesus Christ.* He used two words that are as familiar as they could get: grace and peace. Christianity is a religion of grace. This word is repeated countless times in Bible passages, sermons, and hymns. "Amazing Grace" has to be one of the most sung and beloved songs in all the church. Peace is something that we long for and strive for, especially in a world so torn by violence.

However, as is often the case with words we use so frequently, the depth of meaning behind them is often lost. Grace is so much more than the acrostic: **G**od's **R**iches **A**t **C**hrist's **E**xpense. Peace is so much more than the absence of war. The Philippians would have heard some very profound truths in this blessing from Paul.

The pronouncing of grace, the Greek *charis* or *xaris,* upon someone in New Testament times was often done as part of a farewell or commissioning of people who were taking the gospel to others. It also was a way to call people to stand strong in times of persecution. "Paul's use of *xaris* in his greeting indicates a prayerful concern (the element of intercession is present in the greetings) for the readers. He desires that the Philippians may comprehend more fully the grace of God in which they already stand (cf. Rom 5:2). At the same time he is perhaps commissioning his readers 'to renewed Christian living under the grace appropriate to the immediate circumstances'." (O'Brien1991, 51).

Paul combines this pronouncement of grace with one of peace, the Greek *eirene.* The Hebrew is the more commonly known word *shalom.* The peace of God is far more than the absence of war. Even though that was the primary understanding in Greek culture, we must remember that the first converts in the church in Philippi were the people of Lydia's household. Lydia was at the Jewish prayer time when she met Paul. The Jewish contingent within the church would have heard "peace" and taken its meaning far beyond the absence of war. *Shalom* is about a relationship with God that is one of well-being, contentment, and harmony. Peace is about a relationship of forgiveness and reconciliation. All is well in one's world when one is at peace with God.

> All is well in one's world when one is at peace with God.

So Paul is saying to the Philippians that he wants them to stand strong in the Lord, under His grace, living under that grace, and taking it with them into the world. He also wants them to find peace, no matter what is going on around them, because they have peace with God. If you are in a right relationship with God then everything else will find its proper place in your life. Even if things are going badly and you are under external pressures, you can be at peace because of what you have received through the Lord Jesus Christ.

And the Philippians were facing some outside pressure. They were living in a town that honored Caesar as a god, even calling Him Christ or Savior. The pressure to sacrifice to the emperor would have been immense at times. One's loyalty and patriotism would have been questioned if one did not follow the public religion of honoring the emperor. Paul, in something as generic as a greeting, is encouraging the Philippians to stand fast in the gospel, and not give in to the pressures of emperor worship. They can do this because God is their Father, no matter what the emperor says. And they can do this because Jesus is the Christ, not the Emperor Nero.

The use of Christ would have been understood as a title for Jesus and not as His surname. *Christos* is the Greek word for Messiah. Messiah comes from Hebrew and means the anointed one. It is commonplace for people today to equate Messiah with Savior, thereby mentally limiting the work of the Savior to the forgiveness of our sins; but for the first century Christian, the titles Messiah and Christ would have been equated with *King*. It was the King who was anointed, just like David was anointed by the prophet Samuel. The Jews who were waiting for a Messiah were waiting for one who would come in the line of King David and once again establish the kingdom. Paul was reminding the Philippians that even though they lived in a Roman colony, and even though some of them may be Roman citizens and veterans of the Roman legions, they had a King in Jesus who has given them grace and peace unlike anything Nero could ever offer. It is Jesus, the Messiah, the Christ, who is the anointed One of God and the King of all.

Far from this being a message of hardship, Paul gives them this reminder as a message of hope and joy. Because Christ was their King, they could have grace and peace. Because God the Father has set them apart for His purposes, they could have joy, abundant joy. Even though they faced pressure from without—pressure to conform to their society and the cultural norms around them, they could be assured that their Christ was above all others and the joy of the Lord was theirs to embrace.

WHAT IT MEANS FOR US

We Need *More* Leaders

Church- and pastor-bashing have become a common practice these days. This should be expected from those *outside* the body of Christ, but I am not referring to them. Instead, this habit has become far too commonplace *within* the body of Christ. Some of it comes from those who see any leadership structure as antithetical to their understanding of Scripture, especially their view on the priesthood of all believers. To be sure, church leaders often make themselves easy targets for bashing: from sex scandals to money scandals to the use of abusive, bullying tactics, there is no lack of ammunition readily at hand to take potshots at bad church leaders.

Because such bad leadership is a reality in the church, I have heard speakers at conferences and authors of books say that all we need is the Holy Spirit. They use a very spiritual tone when they speak of this. We don't need to follow men, they say, because men will fail us. Men will lead us astray. Men will abuse and hurt. Many of these same folks have been quick to list the long history of abuses they have suffered at the hands of poor church leaders. Mega-church pastors are particularly targeted in these presentations, but I suspect this may be simply because they are more well-known. I won't comment too much on the irony of these speakers and authors who decry leadership and push for an elimination of it, while they have their own rabid followers and are exercising a whole other type of leadership themselves.

What has become evident to me is that the issue is not that we should not have leaders, the issue is that we need the *right kind* of leaders. There have been too many bad leaders whose conduct has given people a handy excuse to flee church, and then attack anything of structure as institutionalist, or worse, man-made religion wedded to paganism, and not Christianity at all. However, the answer to bad leadership is not the elimination of leadership. The answer to bad leadership is good, godly, Christlike leadership instead.

The Bible in all its unvarnished honesty tells stories of good leaders and bad ones. In the lists of kings in 2 Chronicles, you can read about kings like Asa and Jehoshaphat, who did their best to follow the ways of the Lord and were good kings. You can also read of kings like Ahab and his son, Ahaziah, of whom 2 Chronicles 22:3-4 says this:

He also walked in the ways of the house of Ahab, for his mother was his counselor in doing wickedly. He did what was evil in the sight of the Lord, as the house of Ahab had done. (2 Chronicles 22:3-4)

There were good leaders and there were bad leaders, even then. The answer to bad leaders is to correct them or remove them, and then replace them with good and godly leaders. That is what we find at the opening of Philippians. Paul and Timothy see themselves as slaves to Christ and by extension, slaves or servants to the body of Christ as well. They exist, not for their own position and comfort, but for the sacrificial ministry they offer Christ and His people.

Jesus was confronted with a request by the mother of James and John to grant her sons positions of leadership in Jesus' kingdom in Matthew 20. She wanted not just any positions of leadership, but the seats to the right and left of Jesus when He took up His throne. Jesus proceeded to give a lesson in servant leadership. He contrasts the bad leadership of the Gentiles to the good leadership needed in His kingdom. Gentile leaders lorded their positions and privileges over their followers. In other words, they were overbearing, demanding, unreasonable, and self-seeking leaders. Jesus did not advise that the answer to this problem was no leadership. He said instead that a different kind of leadership was necessary: a leadership that served others and took the form of a servant.

It is servant leadership that Paul and Timothy are exhibiting in the opening salutation of this letter. They are claiming for themselves the position of slaves: slaves to Jesus and His people. None of the audience listening to this letter being read would have thought that Paul was abdicating leadership. They knew the kind of leader he was. He could be strong and demanding when he needed to be, but never for his own benefit. It was always for the sake of the gospel and the people of Christ.

Leaders in the church today need to see that their position of leadership exists for the sake of Christ and the church, and not for themselves. There is a scene from the movie *Braveheart* in which William Wallace, the up-and-coming leader of the Scottish rebellion against the English, confronts the Scottish nobles. The nobles had been compromised because the English have granted them English titles and lands; as a result, the terrible state of the common Scotsman is not something they are willing to improve. That would require risking their own titles and lands. Wallace confronted them brilliantly when he declared, "There's a difference between us. You think the people of this land exist to provide you with position. I think your position exists to provide those people with freedom, and I go to make sure that they have it!"

It is so easy to have our heads turned by the trappings of leadership and the praise that people heap upon leaders. It becomes a slippery slope that many begin to descend. They begin to believe the things flattering followers say about them. Then they begin to feel entitled to position, power, riches and more. It is this slope that recently led one American pastor to request donations, so he could purchase a 65 *million* dollar business jet! In what universe does any pastor think that this is a perfectly reasonable request to make? Only in a world where leadership becomes a means to fulfill one's own pleasure, and not for the sacrificial service of others.

If you are a leader on any level within the body of Christ, then the self-identification of Paul and Timothy as *douloi,* slaves of Christ Jesus and His body, should be your focus in life. If bad leaders have hurt you, the answer is not to abandon the church, and abandon having someone provide leadership in your life. Jesus has established the church and a leadership structure within it for the sake of the body and for His glory. What you need to do is keep looking until you find a good leader, a servant leader, a *doulos.*

We Need *More* Saints

I am not attempting to dismantle the Roman Catholic practice of naming saints. This isn't the place, nor do I have the time and pages for that discussion, but I will say this about the unintended consequences of naming certain people as saints: It lets everyone else off the hook. Here is what I mean by that. The recognition of some people as saints because of their extraordinary lives and miraculous achievements may inspire some to reach higher levels of holiness, but my observation is that, by and large, it causes most people to assume they can't attain to such heights, and therefore, they don't try. Most people assume they could never do what St. Francis of Assisi did, or St. Benedict or even Mother Theresa, who seems destined for sainthood, so they settle for a life of spiritual mediocrity, hoping that God grades on a curve.

Yet here is Paul saying that all followers of Christ are saints, set apart for God's purposes. If you are a follower of Christ, then you are by definition a saint. You have been called by God to serve Him and those around you in His name. You are called to be a difference-maker. We need more people who understand that they have a divine purpose.

In the previous section, I said we needed more leaders and we do, but there is an unintended consequence of the leadership structure within the Protestant world (both the mainline and evangelical branches). There is a strong tendency to elevate our leaders, pastors, ministers, bishops, and whatever else we call them, to near sainthood.

I have seen people claim the church didn't care for them when they were in the hospital. Never mind that a dozen members of the church, including deacons and elders, visited and prayed with that person. If the pastor didn't show up, even though he was away on vacation, then the "church" didn't care. Somehow the idea has taken root that ministry by an ordained pastor is what counts and the ministry of the rest of the body is somehow deficient. Of course, some of the blame for this must rest with the pastors who have held so tightly to their place of special holiness and ministry; but what does it say about the value we place on the ministry of the rest of the saints, if we think that somehow the only real ministry is that performed by ordained clergy?

In the evangelical branch of the faith, we elevate great preachers, calling them the anointed ones as if they are the only ones who get a word from God. We hang on their every word and swear by them, often without really checking the Scriptures for ourselves. That is until they crash and burn; then we find all sorts of reasons why they are charlatans. What does such hero worship say about the role of the Holy Spirit in speaking to, and through, any of the saints?

What we need are *more saints*: people who recognize the gifts God has given them to serve Him and who believe they are called by God to something special. That something may be that you love and serve the people who live on either side of you and do so sacrificially for years, just so they can see and feel the love of Christ and come to faith in Him. You may not preach to thousands in a stadium. That's OK because that stadium preacher will never show up in your neighborhood and take a bowl of soup to your sick neighbor or cut the lawn of the elderly woman across the way. However, that is what saints do *and we need more of them!* They live lives that are different than the norm, lives set apart for service to God in any and every circumstance of life.

We Need *More* Grace and Peace

It is hard to be joyful if you are anxious, unsettled, ill at ease, and scared. All those things become roadblocks to the mission of making disciples that we have all been set apart to achieve. Anxiety and fear have a way of spreading. Fortunately, so do grace and peace.

Paul pronounced a blessing of grace and peace on the Philippians as gifts from God. Throughout the letter, in fact throughout all his writings, Paul emphasizes what we have and are is because we are in Christ. We have grace in abundance because we are in Christ. We have peace that passes all understanding because we are in Christ. The way of grace and peace is through Christ and in Christ. Accessing that grace and peace is not an automatic thing that comes to us without effort. To be sure we are saved by grace and that it is not a work of our own so we cannot boast (Ephesians 2:8-9). Yet in our ongoing life as followers of Christ, we can—and should—grow in grace and in peace (2 Peter 3:18, Romans 14:19, Philippians 4:7-9).

The more we lean into our relationship with Christ, the more we grow in grace and peace. It is through Christ that we have peace, *shalom*, with God. It is through Christ that we receive grace. That is at least part of the reason Paul so often stresses being *in Christ*. It is in our relationship with Jesus that we can grow in grace and peace and in the knowledge of God. That takes effort on our part: effort to keep from straying away and effort to draw nearer to Jesus all the time.

There will be more to say about this as we move deeper into the letter. It will become especially relevant when we reach Philippians 2:12 when Paul urges that we work out our salvation with fear and trembling. On the one hand, grace and peace are clearly a gift from God, as is our salvation. Yet on the other hand, there is a responsibility on our part to do all we can to grow in that grace and peace, and to live out our salvation to the fullest.

Jesus promised that He would be with us always, even to the end of the age (Matthew 28:20), and He promised that we would have His peace with us at all times (John 14:27). Those two are intimately connected. You cannot have the peace of Christ if you do not have Christ. You cannot know His grace if you do not know Him. The more time you spend with Jesus—in His Word, in prayer, worshiping Him, and serving others in His name—the more you will know Him and experience His presence, and the more you will have His peace and know His grace.

When you have that peace and grace, then you are better equipped to go into the world as Paul urged the Philippians to do with his blessing. Then you have something to give the world. It is something of a cliché but nevertheless very true: You cannot

> You cannot give what you do not have.

give what you do not have. You cannot give the message of grace and peace to the world, if you do not have it in your own life. Followers of Christ need more grace and peace because the world is in such desperate need of both.

CHAPTER 2

PRAYING WITH JOY

[3] I thank my God in all my remembrance of you, [4] always in every prayer of mine for you all making my prayer with joy, [5] because of your partnership in the gospel from the first day until now. [6] And I am sure of this, that he who began a good work in you will bring it to completion at the day of Jesus Christ. [7] It is right for me to feel this way about you all, because I hold you in my heart, for you are all partakers with me of grace, both in my imprisonment and in the defense and confirmation of the gospel. [8] For God is my witness, how I yearn for you all with the affection of Christ Jesus. [9] And it is my prayer that your love may abound more and more, with knowledge and all discernment, [10] so that you may approve what is excellent, and so be pure and blameless for the day of Christ, [11] filled with the fruit of righteousness that comes through Jesus Christ, to the glory and praise of God. (Philippians 1:3-11)

WHAT THIS MEANT TO THEM

An Assurance That Paul and Jesus Had Not Forgotten Them

The affection Paul felt for the Christ-followers in Philippi was strong and deep and oozed out of him and into the words of his letter. He prayed for them with joy, holding them in his heart, yearning for them with all the affection of Christ. These words border on being a love letter, which in many ways this is. There is a great love between Paul and the Philippians that is found in no other church with which Paul was connected. Hearing such affection must surely have warmed the hearts of the Philippians and begun to calm the concerns they had for Paul and his situation.

The opening line of this section is somewhat difficult to understand. Is Paul saying that he thanked God for the Philippians in every prayer that he prayed? Or is he saying that he thanked God for the Philippians every time he prayed *for them*? They understood this to mean that Paul prayed for them often; and that every time he did so, he prayed with thanksgiving to God for them, and that when did so, he did it with great joy (Fee1995, 80). That joy was based on their partnership with him in the spreading of the gospel and in the assurance Paul had that God would bring to completion the good work that He has started in the lives of the Philippians and the church.

It was this gospel partnership that was so central in the relationship between Paul and the Philippians, and this was in spite of the fact that his initial stay among them was short! When he left the city after receiving a profuse apology from the city magistrates, the fledgling church at Philippi immediately began to financially support his work and the spread of the gospel. Even now, they still supported him and Paul was mindful to thank them for their recent financial support (4:10-20). Part of what the Philippians would have heard in these words was the affirmation that they were vital to the spread of the good news, and that their efforts blessed Paul beyond measure.

The second reason for Paul's thankfulness and joy was the promise that God would continue to be with the Philippians, and also continue the work in their lives that began when they heard the gospel and came to faith in Jesus. Such an assurance was welcomed by the Philippians who were well aware of their low status in a Roman colony, and of the fact that they were living counter to the culture that so openly honored and worshiped the emperor. There were times when anxiety and consternation gripped the young church in Philippi. Being such an obvious minority made for times of doubt, and feelings of isolation and loneliness. In the face of all that, Paul reminded them that God was with them, and that He had a plan for them, and that His plan, once begun, would be brought to completion at the day of Christ.

It is part of the human condition to need to know that we are making progress, that we are not alone, and that there is an end goal in sight. People can endure some of life's most painful and difficult challenges, as long as they know they are not striving in futility, not alone, and not engaged in a hopeless, never-ending struggle. Paul's words to the Philippians would have reminded them that none of this was true in their case. God was with them. God was in charge. God had a plan and nothing—no principality or power, not even the emperor—could stand against that plan.

The end date for completion of the plan and work that God was doing in their lives (and in the world in general) is the day of Jesus Christ. There is a coming day that is the consummation of all things. That day of Christ would mark the completion of the transformation that was begun in them at their conversion. They had been growing in holiness and Christlikeness. On that day, their transformation would be complete. It is a day to long for and yearn to see.

It is also the day in which, as the Apostle's Creed says, "He will come to judge the living and the dead." And although the creed had not been formulated yet, these Philippians understood that concept. One day Jesus would come as Judge. For the Philippians, this was a divine comfort. Contrary to modern fears of the judgment of God and a coming apocalypse, the Christians in the early decades of the church regarded the day of Christ Jesus (or day of the Lord) as the Old Testament called it, with hope. They viewed it as a day of vindication when the Judge of all the earth would make things right (Revelation 19:1-5). All the suffering they endured, no matter how minor or intense, was certain to end at that time. All would be put to right when Jesus returned and consummated the kingdom He inaugurated during His incarnation.

The Affection Which Paul and Jesus Had for the Philippians

Paul truly loved the Philippians, gushing over them from the opening words of the letter. They felt the force of those words as the letter was being read to them. In verse 7, Paul justified his affection for them and expressed it even more. Lest anyone question the exuberance of Paul's feelings for them, he says this: "It is right for me to feel this way." Given the relationship Paul had with the church and the strong history they shared, it is not unreasonable that Paul felt as he did. In fact, quite the opposite, if Paul did not have such affection for them, we would probably question Paul's heart and motives.

But it was right for him to have such affection, and to hold them in his heart because of the grace of the gospel, and their participation with him in it. That participation began with their conversions and united them with Paul in a way that nothing else could. They may have been a disparate group of people in the beginning: a wealthy businesswoman, a Roman jailer, Jews, Greeks, slaves, freemen, and rich and poor, but they were all one in Christ as a result of the grace of God that brought salvation to them as individuals. They were now a new family. They were Paul's brothers and sisters in the grace of Christ.

The term "the grace they shared" meant more than being united in a common faith though. Paul mentioned in verse 7 that they had some share in grace with him—both in his imprisonment and in the defense and confirmation of the gospel. The defense and confirmation of the gospel is easier to understand than the grace they shared with him in his imprisonment. The answer to sharing in the gospel was in their actions: they worked locally in Philippi to spread the gospel, as Paul did elsewhere. This was "a sharing together" in the overall task of the gospel.

But how did they partake of the grace *of his imprisonment*? Gordon Fee points out two possibilities (Fee1995, 92-93). One idea is that some of them were also being imprisoned for the sake of the gospel. This "same struggle" that Paul says some of them are going through may point to this possibility, but the evidence for that is thin. It is more likely, according to Fee, that this is a reference to the financial assistance that was recently sent to Paul through the visit of Epaphroditus.

The gift was a grace received by Paul from the Philippians; it demonstrated their participation with him in the defense and proclamation of the gospel.

There may be a third connection that the Philippians would have understood by this term. Paul's theology included an understanding of the body of Christ and its interconnectedness to be such that when one part suffered they all suffered, and when one part was honored, they were all honored (1 Corinthians 12:26). In this light, Paul's imprisonment and suffering for the gospel was something that the Philippians experienced vicariously. They were so connected to Paul in heart and spirit that his suffering became theirs. He knew they felt this way about him because of the history they had, which was reinforced by the visit from Epaphroditus and the gift he brought. What the Philippians would have heard is that Paul was encouraged by their connection to him; and that even though he was a prisoner in Rome, he had experienced God's grace because they had reached out to him and let him know that he was not alone. Thus Paul's words are words of thanksgiving and appreciation for the ministry extended to him by the brothers and sisters in Philippi.

Such love on their part for Paul, such participation in the ministry of the gospel, only served to make his affection and yearning for them all the stronger. He ached to see them once again. His affection for them was not only a human affection, but one that found its source in Jesus Christ:

I yearn for you all with the affection of Christ Jesus.
(Philippians 1:8)

So Paul was saying that not only did he yearn for all the Philippians, he also yearned for them with the *all the affection* found in Christ Jesus. That is a lot of affection. The affection that Jesus has for His people drove Him to accept the cross. This was the same affection that drove Paul in His desire to see the Philippians once more. Paul did not have to muster up from his own personal reserve of love for these people. The love he had for them existed solely because of the work Christ Jesus was doing in and through him. Paul loved the Philippians in (and because of) Christ.

Paul continued to pray for the Philippians and it was this affection *in Christ* that fueled his prayer. He prays for them to have this same love for one another, and that this love may grow more and more with each passing day. For a group of diverse people who are learning to live together while on a mission for Christ, this is a call to unity—no matter what the circumstances. While the Philippians certainly did not suffer from the kinds of disunity and strife evident in churches like Corinth, there were still some cracks beginning to appear. Paul's repeated calls to consider others and become servants to one another and not complain and grumble (Philippians 2:3, 2:14), to imitate Christ's humility in the process (Philippians 2:5-10), as well as the call for Euodia and Syntyche to reconcile any differences they have (Philippians 4:2) all indicate that while the unity in Philippi was strong, there was still room for improvement and Paul wanted to see them love even more.

The love Paul prayed for was not some sentimental, emotional response, void of understanding. He prayed that knowledge and discernment would characterize their love for one another. "For the true growth of Christians is when they progress in knowledge and understanding and in love" (Calvin1965, 232). This knowledge is not just any kind of knowledge (Carson1996, 20). It is knowledge of God. In order to love God more deeply, we must know Him more intimately. Love requires a knowledge of the beloved. Paul wanted the Philippians' knowledge of God to grow so that their love for Him, and ultimately their love for one another, could also grow.

> In order to love God more deeply, we must know Him more intimately.

The discernment or understanding that Paul prayed for was also essential. Knowledge as bits of information, as random facts, is not enough to cause love to grow. One must know what the significance of that knowledge is, and what to do with it. As James 2:19 points out, even demons have a correct knowledge of the nature of God and who God is, but they do not have the discernment or wisdom to use that knowledge properly. So the Philippians are being called to a deeper knowledge of God and an understanding of the significance of that knowledge, in order to love God and one another more deeply.

However, this knowledge, love, and discernment are not the end goal. Verse 10 provides a "so that" to Paul's prayer. Paul wants then to grow in love, knowledge, and discernment so that they may *"approve what is excellent, and so be pure and blameless for the day of Christ."* Paul comes back around to the coming judgment. He wants the Philippians to be so conformed into the image of Christ (Romans 8:28-29) that they will be able to stand blameless and unashamed, when Christ comes to judge the living and the dead.

The way to be assured of this is to be filled with the fruit of righteousness (Philippians 1:10), having a life that is guided by the Holy Spirit into a right relationship with Christ. It is only through being in Christ that true righteousness is possible. Paul will recount in chapter 3 that he strove for righteousness on his own more than most and learned the futility of that striving. The freedom that he found in Christ and the righteousness that was granted him by Christ was what he really needed. That is not to say there was no effort or responsibility on our part to live righteously. There is certainly a responsibility for us to live for Christ. That is why Paul prayed for the Philippians that they would stay true to the calling of Christ and live for Him.

He caps this all with the reminder that their lives of righteousness have the purpose of bringing glory to God. What a provocative thought for people who lived for the glory of Rome. Soldiers who knew well the glory of victory and the splendor of Rome are being told to live for the glory of Another. Instead of glorifying a conquering general with a triumph in Rome, they are told to glorify God with lives of righteousness. They are to live, not to bring glory to Rome or Caesar, but to God the Father and the Lord Jesus Christ instead. Paul reminded them that their loyalties lay first and foremost with Christ: Christ crucified, buried, risen, and coming again in glory and triumph.

WHAT IT MEANS TO US

Thankful Prayer and the Spread of the Gospel

When Paul prayed, he did so with incredible thanksgiving. His prayer does not exude some general sense of being thankful for a nice life, much like often happens during the Thanksgiving holiday in the US. Rather Paul is specifically thankful for people and the impact they have had on his life and on the spread of the gospel. How different would your prayer life be if a vast amount of it was taken up with thanking God for specific people in your life, and for the impact they have had on you, and for their efforts in spreading the gospel? Do you spend most of your prayer time asking for things you do not have? Prayer focused on gratitude for what God has already given you could revolutionize your relationship with God, and those He has placed in your life.

It would immediately change your requests. Paul's gratitude for the Philippians led directly into praying for them to be blessed *even more* than they already were. His request was that God would increase the Philippians' love, knowledge, and discernment. Paul did this for the sake of the Philippians, so they would stand firm before Christ on the day of the Lord, knowing their lives had been spent for God's glory. In all this praying, Paul has yet to pray for anything for himself. His prayer life is other-focused.

His prayer life is also focused on the proclamation of the gospel. Paul is grateful for the Philippians, in part because of their partnership with him in the defense and proclamation of the gospel. They have supported him from the beginning in the endeavor that drives his life, the gospel of Jesus Christ, the good news of salvation by faith.

Paul cared passionately about the spread of the gospel for at least two reasons: He agonized over the fate of lost people. We see this most dramatically in Romans 10:1 where Paul cries out that his heart's desire is to see his fellow Jews come to faith in Christ. We see it again in 1 Corinthians 9:20-23 when he says that he became *all things* to *all men* in order that *by any means,* he might bring some to faith in Christ. Paul was willing to do whatever it took, and weather whatever hardship, rejection, pain, abandonment, or suffering that came his way, just for the chance to have others come to a saving knowledge of Jesus Christ. Even his current imprisonment, as we shall see, was viewed as one more chance to tell people about Jesus.

The second reason Paul was so focused on the spread of the gospel was that the gospel was the message of Jesus Christ. It is the good news of what Jesus had accomplished. That good news served to glorify Christ, and Paul was all about bringing glory to Jesus Christ. We don't often think of spreading the gospel in terms of bringing glory to Christ, but that is exactly what it did then and continues to do today. Think about stories of those who received the Congressional Medal of Honor. The very name itself says something. The medal is intended to honor, or glorify, someone for their actions. It is only given to heroes who have earned it through some amazing act of courage. Everyone who receives one has the story of their actions written down and recited when they receive that medal. It is an important

> The story of Jesus had to be told in order to honor and glorify Him.

part of the honor. The story needs to be told. Paul saw the spread of the gospel in the same way. The story of Jesus had to be told in order to honor and glorify Him.

Our efforts at spreading the gospel are often hindered because we allow our concerns for ourselves to take precedent over those of the lost. Our own discomfort, fear of rejection, desire to maintain tranquility at all costs, and the need to avoid conflict becomes more important than the eternal destiny of other human beings. Paul looked at lost people, and his heart ached for them to know Jesus and the freedom that comes in Christ. Paul actually believed that without Jesus those people were condemned to hell, and that he could (and should) do something about that! Unlike Paul, we love ourselves and the lives we have constructed more than we love people who are going to hell without Jesus.

The second motivation, bringing glory to Jesus, is nearly non-existent in any current discussion about spreading the gospel. Yet it should be *central* to our motivation. We often think of bringing glory to God through corporate worship gatherings or living a holy life; but if we go back to our Medal of Honor illustration, we can begin to grasp how telling Jesus' story, the good news of what He did for us, is a fantastic way to bring Him glory. What better way to glorify Christ than to tell of the wonders of His giving up heaven to come to earth as a man, even a servant, who willingly endured torture and crucifixion for our salvation? Nothing tops that!

Revelation is filled with scenes of angels and martyrs and saints gathered around the throne, worshiping the Lamb who was slain (Revelation 4:8-11, 5:6-10, 15:1-4, 19:6-8). The telling of the deeds of the Lamb are intended as *worship of the Lamb*. When we tell others about Jesus and His sacrifice, we glorify Him. Any parent who brags on their children is doing the same thing. We tell of the great deeds of our children, in order to praise them and have others praise them. How much more should we be concerned with telling of the great deeds of our Lord, so that others will also praise Him too?

Paul was so deeply committed to this because he was very aware of his own sin before coming to Christ. He knew that without Christ's saving grace, he would also have been destined for hell. He wanted to glorify Jesus by telling others his story because he loved Jesus so much.

How much do you love Jesus? How much do you love your neighbor? Jesus said that there is no more important command than to love the Lord your God with all your heart, mind, soul, and strength, and to love your neighbor as yourself (Matthew 22:34-40). Evidence of the strength of that love is found in our willingness to spread the gospel and tell others about Jesus. It may sound like a harsh judgment to say that your willingness to spread the gospel is directly proportional to your obedience to the Great Commandment, but it is nevertheless true. Often we focus on the Great Commission (Matthew 28:18-20) as evidence of our maturity in Christ. While that is an important text to measure ourselves against, I contend that it is the Great Commandment that takes precedence. If we truly follow the Great Commandment, the Great Commission will naturally be fulfilled.

CHAPTER 3

JOY IN THE FACE OF DEATH

[12] I want you to know, brothers, that what has happened to me has really served to advance the gospel, [13] so that it has become known throughout the whole imperial guard and to all the rest that my imprisonment is for Christ. [14] And most of the brothers, having become confident in the Lord by my imprisonment, are much more bold to speak the word without fear. [15] Some indeed preach Christ from envy and rivalry, but others from good will. [16] The latter do it out of love, knowing that I am put here for the defense of the gospel. [17] The former proclaim Christ out of selfish ambition, not sincerely but thinking to afflict me in my imprisonment. [18] What then? Only that in every way, whether in pretense or in truth, Christ is proclaimed, and in that I rejoice. Yes, and I will rejoice, [19] for I know that through your prayers and the help of the Spirit of Jesus Christ this will turn out for my deliverance, [20] as it is my eager expectation and hope that I will not be at all ashamed, but that with full courage now as always Christ will be honored in my body, whether by life or by death. [21] For to me to live is Christ, and to die is gain. [22] If I am to live in the flesh, that means fruitful labor for

me. Yet which I shall choose I cannot tell. [23] *I am hard pressed between the two. My desire is to depart and be with Christ, for that is far better.* [24] *But to remain in the flesh is more necessary on your account.* [25] *Convinced of this, I know that I will remain and continue with you all, for your progress and joy in the faith,* [26] *so that in me you may have ample cause to glory in Christ Jesus, because of my coming to you again.* (Philippians 1:12-26)

WHAT THIS MEANT TO THEM

Paul's imprisonment was a painful reality to the Philippians. Even though it appeared that Paul had some freedom as a Roman citizen and was only under house arrest, yet he was still chained to a Roman guard, and they had no certainty of the fate that awaited him. Death was a very real possibility. One could never be sure of how a trial would go, especially when the judge was someone as unpredictable as Emperor Nero.

This passage conveyed Paul's absolute delight over the way the gospel was spreading due to his chains. They were understandably worried about Paul's fate, but Paul was only concerned about the fate of the gospel and the people who got to hear it because he was imprisoned. *Be encouraged by this*, Paul told them. *This has all really turned out rather well. Because I am imprisoned, the entire Imperial (or Praetorian) Guard has heard the gospel!* They had to have received this news with mixed emotions. On the one hand, Paul was still in chains and awaiting his fate. On the other, this most Roman of colonies with its strong ties to Roman veterans was learning that the most elite unit of all, the Praetorian Guard, was hearing the gospel.

Yes, this was a difficult situation that Paul faced, but no one could have anticipated that the result would be the spread of the gospel into one of the most elite military units in Rome, one that served as the personal guard to the emperor. The encouragement that the Word was spreading that far—to people of amazing power and influence—was music to the ears of the Philippians. One can only imagine the rejoicing that went on in their gathering as this letter was read.

But wait, there was more! Other brothers had become even bolder in spreading the gospel as a result of Paul's imprisonment. At first, this seemed to make no sense. One would have imagined that other preachers would have been afraid, shrinking back from proclaiming the gospel, but no! It was expected that they would think: *Wow! If Paul is under arrest for the gospel and possibly facing death, what could happen to us? Maybe we should be more careful in what we say and to whom we say it!* But the opposite happened. The other brothers that Paul mentioned were actually taking courage, seemingly inspired by Paul's situation. The thinking probably went like this: *If Paul is willing to share the gospel with his Roman guards while facing possible death, then maybe I should be willing to share it more in my freedom! If Paul is going to be that courageous, then maybe I need to step up my game and tell others about Jesus too!*

This must have had a similar impact on the Philippians too: *If people are willing to share the gospel message that Jesus is the Christ in the very capital of the empire, then why couldn't we do a better job of sharing it in a Roman colony?* Whatever pressure they may have been feeling as a result of being countercultural, surely could not be as serious as they thought, even here so close to the center of emperor worship.

Paul rejoiced over this spread of the gospel and wanted the Philippians to be encouraged and rejoice over it as well, but he also acknowledged that some of those who have become bold in their preaching were not motivated by the same concern for the lost or God's glory that led him.

Some indeed preach Christ from envy and rivalry....thinking to afflict me in my imprisonment. (Philippians 1:15-17)

This had to be a disturbing note for the Philippians. Their beloved brother Paul was in prison for the defense of the gospel, and some other brothers were trying to make his imprisonment a greater torment than it already was! But how could the preaching of the gospel result in torment for Paul?

Paul wrote that some preached out of envy and rivalry. It must be noted, however, that they were still preaching the gospel. These were not false teachers. They were brothers in Christ preaching the gospel. However, their reasons for doing so were not pure. The ESV uses the words "envy" and "rivalry," but closer to the point would have been "envy" and "jealousy" (O'Brien1991, 99). These brothers wished to share some of the acclaim and notoriety that Paul had achieved.

The Philippians would have understood that these brothers were looking to advance their own reputations, especially with Paul in prison. There was a potential leadership vacuum that they could fill. With Paul in prison, they had room to show their capabilities and gain a greater following. These brothers thought this would have a negative impact on Paul.

They assumed that Paul also thought in terms of human following and fame, and would be somewhat depressed to learn that others were perhaps eclipsing him. They assumed that reaction in Paul because that was what mattered to them. Yes, they were preaching the gospel; but in their hearts, the acclaim of men was sweet to their ears. That acclaim seemed like a limited commodity too. Their thinking was that if Paul had a big following, there would not be enough to go around for all. With Paul in prison, the field for them opened before their feet. If they received greater acclaim, that must mean Paul was getting less. *So be it!* they thought. *It's about time.*

But Paul cared nothing for human praise. What mattered to Paul was that the gospel was preached (Philippians 1:18). Even if people preached the gospel from false motives, Paul didn't care. He rejoiced in the spread of the good news of Jesus Christ. *The message was being preached, even while he was encumbered! Praise God!* His situation in prison did not impact his joy. The impure motives of other preachers could not rob him of his joy. The potential of his own death could not steal his joy. In all these circumstances, *the gospel was being preached, and people were coming to faith, and Christ was being glorified!* As far as Paul was concerned, *this was not just good, it was fantastic!*

IT IS ALL ABOUT JESUS

The third paragraph of the text, verses 18b-26, takes the joy over the spread of the gospel one giant step further. This text carries it to the doorstep of death and Paul's joy over the very real possibility of being found guilty by Nero and beheaded. Paul repeated again that he would rejoice over the spread of the gospel, no matter what, but he could not avoid discussion of his possible future any longer.

On the one hand, he was confident that God would positively answer the prayers being offered regularly and passionately for his deliverance (Philippians 1:19). That deliverance meant that he might have the opportunity to visit them once again. One can almost sense a collective sigh among the congregation at this point. *Paul is thinking it will all turn out well and he will be able to see us again. Hooray!* However, that sigh would have quickly given way to a collective groan. It could also go the other way and result in his death.

Paul eased into this by assuring the Philippians that just as he eagerly expected to be delivered and once again visit them, he also eagerly expected to remain courageous and would honor Christ with his body, no matter what (Philippians 1:20). That was an ominous statement. Paul was preparing himself and the Philippians for either outcome: his deliverance to freedom or his deliverance to the ax. Either way, Paul still intended to glorify Christ. He intended to honor Christ with his body in life or in death.

He followed that intent with one of the most remarkable and memorable statements in the entire Bible:

For me to live is Christ, and to die is gain...Yet which I shall choose I cannot tell. I am hard pressed between the two. (Philippians 1:21-23)

Finally, Paul put all the cards on the table. The Philippians have it plainly set before them. Paul knew life and death hung in the balance, and *he was actually uncertain as to which outcome he preferred.*

The reason for the uncertainty was that both life and death had their benefits to Paul. Both life and death are really all about Christ. To live was to serve Christ with every fiber of his being. To die was to go and be with Christ. Both were a glorious privilege to Paul. He would rejoice over either one. He was so torn by each possibility that he was on the horns of a dilemma, as the proverb goes.

> Both life and death are really all about Christ.

Greek mythology includes the story of Scylla and Charybdis. Scylla was a six-headed sea monster on one side of a narrow strait and Charybdis was a massive whirlpool on the other. In Homer's *Odyssey*, the hero Odysseus is torn between which direction to take as he sails his ship through the strait. He opts to sail closer to the sea monster, hoping to lose only a few men instead of nearer the whirlpool, which could result in the death of the entire crew, even though it also carried the possibility of escaping the force of the whirlpool altogether, sparing all. It was a tough choice: go in one direction and be certain to have a few deaths or go in another in the hope that there would be no one lost, but risking all. Either way the decision was a choice between two evils. Paul makes it clear that his decision is the opposite. It was a decision between two equally desirable outcomes, but he could only have one.

The Philippians needed to hear that Paul loved them and yearned to be with them. His continuation in this life would allow for that opportunity. But at the same time, they needed to know that if he was executed, he was ready to embrace that. They needed to be told that they should not grieve for him but rejoice, for that is what he would surely be doing in the presence of the Lord.

If Paul was set free and able to return to the Philippians, it would benefit them. In fact, as he wrote, he began to lean in that direction, seeing that as the outcome. One can almost follow his stream of consciousness as he writes:

1. *I know your prayers will turn out for my deliverance (Philippians 1:19).*

2. *But I will not be ashamed if it happens otherwise and will honor Christ in my body even in death (Philippians 1:20).*

3. *Part of me actually desires to die and be with Christ (Philippians 1:23).*

4. *Yet as I think about it more, I know it is better for you that I remain (Philippians 1:24).*

5. *Actually I am convinced that I will remain with you, so that you progress further in the faith (Philippians 1:25).*

The Philippians had a quick rollercoaster ride in those six verses. They went from being certain of Paul's pending freedom to thinking he might be executed and seemed to be longing for that, and then back to anticipating his freedom and return to them! Underneath this emotional turmoil, they heard the strong faith and trust Paul placed in Christ and the assurance he had of the glorious life to come. How heartening this was for them.

They also heard him once again calling them to joy. Paul would remain in order to assist them in their progress in the faith. He could call them to have joy in their faith because he was still rejoicing, even in prison. He was rejoicing that the gospel was being preached with greater boldness *because* he was in prison. He was rejoicing that he might one day see the Philippians again. He was even rejoicing over the prospect of being executed, so he could go be with Jesus! All of Paul's joy was possible because of his relationship with Christ, his faith in Christ, and his assurance that Christ was with him, *no matter what*.

WHAT IT MEANS TO US

Our culture shapes us in ways we rarely recognize and question. When we are confronted with startling ideas that run completely counter to our cultural norms and values, we have an opportunity to examine what we truly hold dear. Paul's joy in the face of death provides us with just such an opportunity.

There are three cultural values in which western Christians are immersed. They are seemingly wonderful values on the surface, but underneath they are destroying our faith. Those values are safety, comfort, and security. Paul's life directly confronts those values and this letter calls us to seriously reconsider what we value and why.

Safety

One of my roles when I was a pastor at Northland Church was to travel and train other pastors across the globe. In any given year I made multiple trips to Africa, Asia, South America, and Eastern Europe, and occasionally led groups of people on various short-term mission trips. Invariably people asked me about safety, and some indicated a hesitancy or outright unwillingness to go overseas because of safety concerns. The rise in tensions presented by radical Muslims only served to accentuate those concerns. Even as I write this, people are reeling from a recent attack by al-Shabaab on Garissa University in Kenya. I have been to Kenya a dozen times or more in the past few years and have trained a few hundred pastors there. Understandably people are asking if this university is anywhere near places I have been and do I know anyone there. The conversation often turns to the possibility of ending trips to Kenya out of concern for our safety.

> You are in more danger if you stay home than if you go where He calls.

Paul would not let such concerns reach the light of day. The call to take the gospel to all the world was not contingent on how safe a place was. In fact, Jesus made it clear that because of Him and the gospel, we would never really be safe from danger. The opposite is true. Because of Him and the gospel, we can expect persecutions and hardship and danger. He promises danger but He also promises to be with us, no matter what. Paul rejoiced in the presence of Christ and was willing to risk the dangers for the sake of the gospel.

The truth of the matter is that if God calls you to a place of some risk for the sake of the gospel, you are in more danger if you stay home than if you go where He calls.

Comfort

Comfort is all the rage. We want comfort in everything. In fact, comfort has become such a strong value in our culture that making someone uncomfortable is tantamount to assaulting them. We want a life void of tension, hardship, struggle, or effort. We want everything to be plush, cozy, and warm. Yet here we have Paul, embracing his arrest and facing execution because it is the best way to move the gospel forward. If you value comfort over sharing the gospel, you never will do it because the gospel, even though it is good news, causes tension and makes people uncomfortable. Spreading the gospel may require you to go places that, while not dangerous, are certainly not comfortable or luxurious.

Security

By security I mean your *financial* security. Baby Boomers in the US are especially concerned about financial security. With so many of them entering retirement, there is much consternation over how long their money will last. The prevailing wisdom is that as long as you have a big enough nest egg of financial resources, then life will be okay. We will see later in Philippians that Paul was content, no matter what the state of his resources, because no matter what he had or did not have, what he always had was Jesus, the assurance of life to come, and a purpose in this life. Financial security is of no concern when you are assured of eternal security with Christ.

The way we approach these values says a great deal about our relationship with Christ. They are not bad values. In fact there are things about them that are good. The problem comes when these (or any values) take priority over Christ *and* what He has called us to as His followers. I emphasize the *and* because we so easily say that Christ is first in our lives, but forget that we show Him as first *by following Him and obeying Him—no matter what*. It is easy to declare what your values are, but the truth of that *is seen*, not heard. What we do shows what we really believe. We might know in our heads that putting Christ first is the correct value. It is the Sunday school answer; but unless we actually live differently, we are fooling ourselves into thinking Christ and proclaiming His gospel are our highest values.

Our values can easily become idols, things we worship without even realizing we are doing so. They become idols when we make decisions in life that put those values ahead of the call Jesus has placed on our lives. For instance, if you decide not to go on a short-term mission trip because you just can't sleep well unless you are in your own bed, or you can't wrap your mind around eating rice and beans for ten days, or any of a host of other discomforts, then you are allowing *comfort* to function as your god instead of Jesus.

THE WORSHIP OF LIFE

If there is one thing we value above all others it is life itself. By life I mean the physical, temporal life that we experience *in the here and now*. Of course, we think of eternal life, or life after death, but the mere fact that we put an adjective to life when we speak of eternal life tells me that when we think of life, we really mean *this life*. This is the life that we want to keep and hold onto *at all costs*. We try to extend it as long as possible. We try to deny the inevitable onward march of time and as we get closer to the end of this life, we go on fad diets, have plastic surgery, and even toy with cryogenics, thinking we can freeze our bodies in the hope of thawing them out some day in the future when a cure for whatever killed us is found.

To be sure, we hope there is something beyond this life. Religions around the world point people to a future hope of some sort. Christians look to the resurrection from the dead and eternal life with Christ, but our actions often betray what we really think of this life and the tenuous hold our faith has on the life to come. The fact that we are so struck by Paul's dilemma of not being sure if he wants to live or die points to how tightly we hold on to this earthly existence and the shallowness of our understanding of eternal life.

Paul was truly torn between the two because he saw such blessed benefits in both. Oddly enough, the benefits are not equally shared. The benefit of remaining alive was not to Paul's benefit. Most of us would think of all the personal reasons we want to remain alive: the things we want to do, the experiences we want to have, or even just avoiding the pain of death. Our bucket list comes to mind. But when Paul thinks of staying, he thinks only of the benefit his life can have towards the Philippians. To remain is more necessary for their benefit: so they may progress and have joy in the faith, and so they may have ample cause to glory in Christ. Staying alive for Paul only makes sense because his life will be used to benefit others in their progress in the faith.

Paul only sees personal benefit in his death. To die would mean to be with Jesus and that is what Paul really longs for. He wants to be with his God. He does not idolize this life. Yes, he enjoys what he does in life—serving others for the cause of Christ, but when push comes to shove, what Paul wants for himself is to go and be with Jesus. This life is only about serving Jesus. The next life is all about being with Jesus in glory.

This life is only about serving Jesus.

There is nothing wrong with enjoying this life. God made it to be good, but the greatest joy we can find in life is to live it in the service of the Lord. Paul delighted in the things of this life because he got to tell people about Jesus and see people grow in their faith and love towards Jesus. Paul took joy in the gospel and the many benefits it showered on others. According to Paul, to live is Christ; to love Christ; to serve Christ, to preach Christ and Him crucified, risen, and coming again. Paul was enraptured with the joy of Christ in this life, but he longed even more so to see Christ face-to-face, to know and be known by Him, free from the ravages of sin, having finally conquered the finally enemy, death.

Paul cherished what he could do in this life, but he held this life loosely. Paul clung to the hope of glory with Jesus with all his might. It causes me to ask (and should cause you to ask) this: "Am I clutching to this life with a faint hope of the life to come, or am I living this life to the fullest, serving Jesus and spreading His Word, while yearning for the life to come?"

CHAPTER 4

PERSEVERING AND SUFFERING WITH JOY

²⁷ *Only let your manner of life be worthy of the gospel of Christ, so that whether I come and see you or am absent, I may hear of you that you are standing firm in one spirit, with one mind striving side by side for the faith of the gospel, ²⁸ and not frightened in anything by your opponents. This is a clear sign to them of their destruction, but of your salvation, and that from God. ²⁹ For it has been granted to you that for the sake of Christ you should not only believe in him but also suffer for his sake, ³⁰ engaged in the same conflict that you saw I had and now hear that I still have. (Philippians 1:27-30)*

WHAT THIS MEANT TO THEM

For all the certainty Paul expressed about being released and able to visit the Philippians in the future, there is still a note of caution in what he wrote in this section. The phrase translated as "only let your manner of life" in our versions does not quite match what the Philippians heard Paul saying as this letter was being read to them. Coming right on the heels of his discussion about life and death and visiting or not visiting them again, the force of the Greek phrase used here is actually: "No matter what happens to me!" "Thus it is as though he had said, 'But the Lord will provide for me; but as for you... Whatever may happen to me, see that you yourselves go forward in the right course'" (Calvin1965, 241). So whether Paul was released and able to visit the Philippians or not, their course should remain the same. They must live the life Christ had called them to live, and that meant a life worthy of the gospel.

The use of "only" (*monon*) at the start of the sentence would have caught the attention of the Philippians. It was saying that there was but *one, single imperative* (one command) to which they must adhere. It had the force of Jesus saying there was one Great Commandment: to love the Lord your God with all your heart, mind, soul, and strength, and your neighbor as yourself. In fact, it can be argued that this sentence *is* the Great Commandment *in different words*. There is one thing above all else that you must do, Paul was saying: *Live your life worthy of the gospel to which Jesus called you.* The way to live most worthy of that gospel would be to love God and your neighbor with all you have and all you are.

> Your lives need to be lived so that the gospel goes forth.

The message to the Philippians was that this life was *all about the gospel.* For Paul to remain in this life would be for the benefit of others—so they would grow in the knowledge of the gospel. Paul told the Philippians this: *Your lives need to be lived so that the gospel goes forth.* Stated in the negative it would be this: *Don't do anything that could in anyway discredit the gospel.* Paul fashions more of this idea later in his letter; but for now, he is calling the Philippians to the ideal of a life worthy of the eternal life they have received by grace.

Paul also appealed to them for his own sake. He wanted to be encouraged by a good report of their lives together. Given the love they had for Paul and the awareness of his current life-and-death situation, one can easily understand that this was an emotional appeal. If Paul were to hear that the Philippians were dishonoring the gospel in some major way, it would have broken his heart. His joy came from their progress in the gospel. To hear that they had fallen backward instead of continuing in God's grace forward would have been more than he could bear, especially during his imprisonment. If he were to be released and able to visit them, and then discovered upon his arrival that they had dishonored the gospel, it would still have been a crushing blow. Having spent all that time in prison for the cause of Christ, only to find out that his beloved Philippians were at one another's throats instead of loving one another would have been a stab in Paul's heart.

Any of the Philippians listening to the reading of this letter would have to have been moved by Paul's appeal. He asked so little for himself and was always willing to sacrifice for others. He had been beaten and jailed in their very city in order to bring the message of salvation to them. How could any of them risk breaking his heart?

LIVING AS ONE

Paul went on to describe what the way forward looked like. Without giving them a command of *how* to live, he very artistically let them know what a life worthy of the gospel looked like by letting them know of his confidence in them to live that out. He told them he knew they would "stand firm in one spirit, with one mind, striving side by side for the faith of the gospel." Living in unity *for* the gospel was to live a life *worthy of the gospel*. It was only in unity, side by side, that they could move the gospel forward.

Paul had heard that, to some degree, there is disunity developing in the church. He would address that head-on in Philippians 2:1-4 when he warned against rivalry and conceit, and again later in Philippians 4:2 when he called out Euodia and Syntyche. However, before addressing the particulars of disunity, Paul reminded them what was at stake: the very gospel of Christ and ultimately the glory of God. Paul lifted their eyes from the worldly concerns of position and status that they were starting to focus on, and directed them instead to the higher, upward calling they had in Christ Jesus. It is a calling that could not be fulfilled if they were not united in heart, mind, and spirit.

Part of the reason they had to be united was that spreading the gospel was hard work. It required that they *strive* together, *side by side.* There is almost a martial spirit in this phrase that would have resonated with the Philippians. How many of them would have pictured Roman legionnaires standing firm, side by side, shields locked, weapons in hand, ready to take on the enemy, confident in the power of their unity? Given the military history of Philippi, it must certainly have crossed the minds of more than a few of them in the church as they listened. After all, it was this strategy that had made Rome the great empire that it was: They maintained the most powerful, disciplined troops in the known world. This same strategy was what it was going to take to move the gospel forward. Every one of them must be united, literally *locked together*, in the unity of the Holy Spirit.

Such unity would give them confidence as they faced the outside enemy. They had opponents (1:28); Paul doesn't describe yet who they are, but certainly the Philippians knew who they were. Gordon Fee does a wonderful job of bringing to light who are the most likely candidates for those opponents: "in light of several hints within the letter, especially the emphasis on Christ as "lord" and "savior", and the loyalty of this colony to the cult of the emperor, it seems very likely that the (Roman) citizens of Philippi, who would have honored the emperor at every public gathering, were putting special pressure on the Philippian believers; their allegiance had now been given to another *kyrios,* Jesus, who had been executed at the hands of the empire" (Fee1995, 167). (*Kyrios* is the Greek word for "lord" which was applied to the Caesars as part of the worship of the emperor.)

This was the same struggle that Paul had and now shares with the Philippians (1:30). Paul had to defend his allegiance to Jesus as Lord in the face of accusations that he was a rabble rouser who was stirring up people in rebellion against Roman ways and Roman rule. Although the Philippians were not imprisoned and facing death as Paul was, they were still engaged in having to stand firm in their faith, knowing that all around them were people who looked on them with suspicion and even disdain.

By connecting their struggle with his own, Paul was affirming the unity that he was calling them to demonstrate. He was standing together with them. He might be in prison in Rome and they might be walking free in Philippi, but they were all together in their defense of the gospel and their unyielding faith in Jesus Christ as Lord and Savior. That put them firmly together, shields locked as it were, standing firm. There had to be some encouragement for the Philippians on hearing this. *Yes, we have opposition. Yes, people who have been friends and colleagues have turned against us, but we are not alone, and together we can and will stand.*

THE FELLOWSHIP OF CHRIST'S SUFFERINGS

Nestled in the midst of these words of unity and encouragement is a phrase that I am sure the Philippians would rather have *not* heard:

> *For it has been granted to you that for the sake of Christ you should not only believe in him but also suffer for his sake. (Philippians 1:29)*

Normally when you are *granted something*, that "thing" is regarded as a positive and desirable item. You are granted a privilege. Getting a land grant means you have been *given* property. Receiving a grant from a foundation means some money is coming your way. The *granting* of things usually equates with good news, but the Philippians heard something in the granting of a privilege that may not have sounded all that wonderful. It was very much a mixed bag instead. It was granted to them to believe in Jesus Christ, and receive all the blessings that came with that: eternal life, a new family here on earth, the joy of the Lord, a new perspective on life, and all the rest. But that granting also brought with it *suffering for the sake of Christ*.

Following Christ can and will be hard. Striving for the sake of the gospel requires effort, sweat, pain, and sometimes death. Paul was encouraging the Philippians with an assurance that they were not alone, that they had the power to stand together, that their unity made them stronger than they realized, and finally, that for the sake of the gospel and the glory of God, they could stand without fear of their opponents. However, all of that was tempered with the equal assurance that suffering would be part and parcel of their striving together for Christ's sake.

The Philippians understood that suffering was a *normal part of the Christian life*, and also that it was *a privilege to suffer* for the cause of Christ. They knew that Paul was not an academic speaking from some lofty, ivory tower. No, Paul knew about real suffering. The jailer had cleansed the wounds from the beating Paul and Silas had unjustly received on their first trip to Philippi (Acts 16:33). That jailer and his household as well as Lydia and hers, along with the young girl released from the clutches of demon possession, had all witnessed the brutality that came from following Christ. They saw how Paul endured, persevered, and even accepted, these hardships.

But this did not deter them from following Christ. Much like the brothers who were emboldened to preach the gospel all the more by Paul's imprisonment in Rome, the Philippians were strengthened by Paul's words and example. Like many other first century Christ-followers, they would have counted it a privilege to suffer for the sake of Christ. Perhaps they had been told, even by Luke himself, of how the first apostles had considered it a privilege to be worthy enough to suffer for Jesus (Acts 5:41).

When you came to faith in Christ in the first century, especially in a Roman colony like Philippi, you were marking yourself as an outsider. Living apart from the norm, they faced ridicule for not acknowledging the many gods of the Greco-Roman world. They faced abuse for believing that the Messiah would have been crucified like a common criminal. Add to that, their firm belief in a bodily resurrection, and they most certainly were held in derision within their culture. In essence, the Philippian Christians were probably a laughingstock to those around them. Even their sanity would have been called into question. Fail to honor the emperor with a sacrificial offering and you risked death. All one needed to do in order to avoid such a fate was compromise just a little: Just keep quiet about Jesus, the crucifixion, and resurrection, and put a pinch of incense on that altar while you're at it.

For the Philippians and many other Christians of this time, the persecution they suffered was a badge of honor. It was a sign that they were living a life worthy of the gospel to which they had been called. It all worked together. No matter what happened to Paul, their focus was to live a life worthy of the gospel by being united in mind and spirit. They were standing together in the assurance of the gospel, shields locked, knowing that they had nothing to be afraid of, regardless of who opposed them. Paul's message was clear: When the suffering comes, as it surely will, rejoice! Rejoice because you know you are living as Christ wants you to live; you are honoring Him with your very bodies, as Paul promised to do too.

WHAT IT MEANS TO US

Christian Lives Matter

In the wake of the deaths of two young black men involved in altercations with police officers, the phrase, "Black Lives Matter" was coined to raise consciousness about this serious issue of black youths dying needlessly in these conflicts. Directly on its heels came the phrase, "Blue Lives Matter" in an effort to shed light on the rate at which police officers were being killed in the line of duty. Not to be left out, "Christian Lives Matter" popped up to make people aware of the mass killings that ISIS was engaged in, apparently trying to rid their part of the world of all the Christians. Eventually, "All Lives Matter" was added to the rest. The positive point of the various campaigns was to show the value of life, and that lives were being wasted through violence; but perhaps the best thing I heard in all of this was someone saying that we need to get beyond the categories, and make it personal. Each of us needs to recognize that "Your Life Matters". Yes, my life matters, whether I am black or a police officer or a Christian. However, I need to believe that no matter who you are, your life matters to me!

Without question, Christians should be concerned about the escalating persecution and murder of Christians around the world, but the heading for this section, "Christian Lives Matter," is not intended as a way to shed light on that tragedy. Rather it is intended to shed light on an entirely different calamity—one that Paul hoped to avoid. That is the tragedy of what happens when the lives of Christians are not lived in a manner worthy of the gospel. Your life as a follower of Christ matters because it can either point people towards Christ or away from Him. These days there is much hand-wringing over the state of the church, evangelical Christian involvement in

> You can make a difference in the world by how you follow Christ.

politics, the Millennial Generation abandoning an orthodox faith, and more. But all of those things are dealing in categories and generalities. We need to make it personal, and recognize that your life as a follower of Christ matters. You can make a difference in the world by how you follow Christ. That especially includes how you approach suffering and hardship.

Christians often make use of the word "witness" to talk about sharing our faith. Some Bible translations use the word "testimony" instead in order to describe telling others about Jesus and sharing the good news. Both "witness" and "testimony" are good words, having connections to the courtroom where a person spoke only of what they knew to be *the truth, the whole truth, and nothing but the truth.* A Christian who witnesses for Christ or gives testimony for Christ is someone who is speaking the truth about Jesus—what they have seen and heard and know to be true (1 John 1:1-3).

The Greek word that is most often translated as either witness or testimony has a rich and deep significance. It is the word *martus,* and is also the root word for "martyr." The significance is that this common root word helps us to see that one's words and one's life are essential for the effective spread of the gospel and to bring glory to Jesus. When an early Christian heard that they were to be a *martus* for Jesus, they understood they were to both speak and live in such a way that they pointed people to Jesus. The ultimate expression of their faith would be to die rather than deny Christ—to become a martyr for their faith in Christ.

St Francis of Assisi is quoted as saying, "At all times preach the gospel; when necessary use words." Lately people have been using this idea to make using words a last resort in sharing of the gospel, trying to make the testimony of our lives foremost. To be sure, there has been a great deal of preaching the gospel by people whose lives run counter to the words; the result of that is that the words fall on deaf ears.

Paul would certainly have called for lives that matched the message, just as we are calling for here. However, the popularity of St. Francis's words reveal a disturbing premise: that somehow the *living* of the gospel is more important than the *speaking* of the gospel.

Being martyred for the faith is undoubtedly the most dramatic way one's life can point people to Jesus, but martyrs usually become martyrs because of the *words* they have spoken. Or in the case of the martyrdom of Christians at the hands of ISIS and al-Shabaab, it is because of the words they *refuse* to say that would deny Christ. Living a life worthy of the gospel requires that we both live a radical lifestyle based on following Jesus *and speak of what we believe*. Why is it necessary to speak? Because according to Scripture unless people *hear* the gospel, how will they believe?

> How then will they call on him in whom they have not believed? And how are they to believe in him of whom they have never heard? And how are they to hear without someone preaching? (Romans 10:14).

Sadly Christians have all too often used their speech to sow discord and disunity in the body of Christ instead. The Internet and social media have served to show that in many respects Christians behave no differently in their attitudes and actions towards one another than non-Christians do. A preacher says something out of order or does something suspect and the blogosphere erupts with condemnation

and venom that matches (or sometimes exceeds) those which surround politics, race, environmental issues, or discussions of gender in
the secular world. The divisiveness that results gives people outside
the camp all the justification they need to stay away from Christians
and church.

How far we are from the prayer of Jesus in John 17 and the words He
prayed, while staring death in the face:

> [20] *"I do not ask for these only, but also for those who will believe in
> me through their word,* [21] *that they may all be one, just as you, Fa-
> ther, are in me, and I in you, that they also may be in us, so that the
> world may believe that you have sent me.* [22] *The glory that you have
> given me I have given to them, that they may be one even as we are
> one,* [23] *I in them and you in me, that they may become perfectly one,
> so that the world may know that you sent me and loved them even
> as you loved me." (John 17:20-23)*

Think for a moment about what Jesus is praying for. He is asking that
His followers would be so united that it would look like the unity He
and the Father have with one another. He is asking that we have an un-
breakable, inseparable unity, one that is solidified by sharing the same
Holy Spirit. There is a gospel reason for that unity. It is not just so we
can enjoy the warm fellowship that comes from unity, or the peace
that is generated by oneness in God's Spirit. Those are both wonderful,
but Jesus prayed that we would be one "so that the world may know
that you sent me and loved *them* as you loved me." Wow! Jesus prayed
that we would be united so that the world would know *that God loves
them and sent Jesus to die for them.*

The degree that the body of Christ is broken and fractured is the degree to which we scuttle our own efforts to share the gospel with the world. Jesus said it as plainly as possible in His prayer: we need to be one so that people will believe that the Father sent the Son to a world He loves. If we cannot love one another then people have little tangible evidence of what the Father's love looks like. If however, people see Christians, mirroring all the diversity that makes up human beings from every tribe, tongue, and nation, actually loving one another, serving one another, and harmoniously united to one another, then they can begin to imagine that maybe, just maybe, they could be loved that way too.

> If we cannot love one another then people have little tangible evidence of what the Father's love looks like.

Having raised three sons, my wife and I have witnessed our share of group dynamics. One of the things we noticed was that our house was often filled with their friends. This was true when they were little: the pool, yard, and house were filled with kids. It was also true as they got older; it was normal to wake up on a Saturday morning and find bodies strewn around the family room and in bedrooms with five or six extra teenage boys.

On the other hand, there were always homes that the gang never spent time in, and didn't go to very often. Those were the homes in which the parents were not getting along. Homes with stress and conflict do not attract kids to come and play. In fact, the ones who live there are usually looking for someplace else to be too. Not that our house was perfect, but kids knew we loved one another, and they found that we loved them too.

The same holds true for the church. Who wants to be part of a family that is always arguing, stressed out, and bickering over things that seem petty at best? Is there a place for disagreement in the body of Christ? Of course there is. Theological truth, purity of life and practices that promote the gospel must be maintained, and that will bring its share of disagreements. But with rare exceptions, it is possible to maintain unity in the Spirit while still disagreeing over these finer points.

At this point in Philippians, Paul was just beginning to broach the subject of unity and how to maintain it. Much more is to come, especially in Chapter 2, as he begins to point us to the example of Christ that will challenge us to put others ahead of ourselves and consider their needs before our own. For now, it is safe to say that how we live our lives matters. It matters for the sake of the integrity of the gospel and for people who need to see Christ in us.

CHECK YOUR PRIVILEGE

Orbiting around the debates over race in America today is the notion of white privilege. I see the same debate taking place on my many trips to South Africa and have had numerous conversations about it with whites and blacks. The phrase is intended to get white people to recognize that they have enjoyed certain advantages simply because they are white. Much of it has to do with how people read history and the impact of a preceding generation's behavior on people alive today. It is a hot debate and causes turbulent emotions to come spilling out all over the place. I don't know that there will ever be agreement as to the true impact of race and privilege on the lives of individuals. I certainly don't see society at large coming to any agreement on a solution anytime soon, but what the discussion does is force us to look at assumptions we didn't even know we had and the situations and perspectives of those who are different from us. This must be the case from both directions—black and white.

I bring this up because there is a certain Christian privilege that needs to be addressed too, especially in the US. Because the United States has been exceptionally friendly towards Christianity for nearly all its history, Christians have come to expect things to be always favorable to Christian ideas and practices. In the last decade or two, that has shifted dramatically. It can easily be argued that acceptance in our society is available to anyone, *except* the evangelical Christian who holds to the exclusive claims of Jesus and a traditional biblical morality.

This seismic shift in the cultural landscape has caused many Christians to cry out in fear and anger over the state of things. While the values of society generally mirrored those of the Bible and we once held the cultural center in our country, now we are marginalized to the rim and risk being pushed off the edge. The reaction of many Christians is one of outrage and disgust at the current state of things. When they are treated in an unfair or unjust manner, the response is one of indignation, protest, and sometimes, actual litigation. People talk about taking back America and cry out to God, wondering why they are being so oppressed. We miss the privileged position Christianity held in our culture.

Having been to places around the world where one risks their life for being a Christian and having dear friends who have been jailed and beaten because of their faith, I find myself both amused and annoyed by the typical American Christian response to suffering and persecution. What we experience in the United States is nothing. It is almost not worth bothering God over.

I would go so far as to say that if we are going to bring our suffering and persecution before God, it needs to be with a completely different attitude. It needs to be one of rejoicing and thanksgiving. Paul said *we should consider ourselves privileged* to be granted a place in the fellowship of Christ's suffering. Rather than complaining about people hating us because we follow Christ, we need to thank God that they noticed, and that we were enough like Christ to be allowed to suffer in His name. Jesus said this:

> *"Blessed are you when others revile you and persecute you and utter all kinds of evil against you falsely on my account." (Matthew 5:11)*

Do you understand what Jesus is saying? Suffering for the cause of Christ is a blessing. We talk about being blessed only when we get a financial benefit, or a promotion at work, or have people throw a party in our honor or any other number of good things that anyone would consider a plus. But Jesus says that we are blessed when we face opposition to our faith. When people call you a homophobe because you are opposed to gay marriage, based on what Jesus said about marriage being between a man and woman, Jesus says you are blessed. When you are called a bigot because you think that the only way to heaven is by trusting in Christ as Lord, then Jesus says you are blessed.

Let's be clear about one thing. You can be persecuted and have people say all sorts of nasty things about you because you love Jesus and stand with Him. You can also face the same accusations because you are basically an angry jerk who happens to believe the same things Jesus taught. *There is a massive difference.* If you love your neighbor as yourself, thus seeking to obey the Great Commandment, and yet find yourself facing vitriol for your faith, then rejoice, count it a blessing. If you have not been loving your neighbor and face that same vitriol, then count it as a warning because you are not representing Christ.

If Christians began to view the push back we get, not as something to resist and push against harder, but as the expected blessed result of following Jesus, we would change the entire tone of the current cultural debate. Even so, let's be wise in how we rejoice. Note that when the apostles were beaten by the Sanhedrin in Acts, they didn't jump up and down with rejoicing in front of them.

Then they left the presence of the council, rejoicing that they were counted worthy to suffer dishonor for the name. (Acts 5:41)

You don't rub it in someone's face. Rather you rejoice and let the joy of the Lord guide you in your interactions with others who do not understand your faith. This became crucial for the early apostles as they faced further arrests and persecution. They dealt with their detractors in a calm, reasoned, yet firm, way. They did not scream, shout, fight back, or scheme for dominance. They simply accepted the honor of being rejected because of Jesus, and they loved their enemies.

The sad fact is that we, as Christians, have become very thin-skinned and hard-hearted when we need to be thick-skinned and tenderhearted. Christians asserting their rights in order to maintain some position of strength within society hardly seems to fit with Jesus' call to pray for people who oppress and persecute you. We have a sense of being denied something we are owed when we face opposition from the world. We sound as though we were entitled to better treatment than we are getting. Missing is the idea that we gain something of inestimable value when we are rejected by the world: we gain admission into the fellowship of Christ's sufferings, and we gain joy in the knowledge that we are counted worthy to suffer for His name.

CHAPTER 5

THE JOY OF SERVING OTHERS

[1] So if there is any encouragement in Christ, any comfort from love, any participation in the Spirit, any affection and sympathy, [2] complete my joy by being of the same mind, having the same love, being in full accord and of one mind. [3] Do nothing from selfish ambition or conceit, but in humility count others more significant than yourselves. [4] Let each of you look not only to his own interests, but also to the interests of others. (Philippians 2:1-4)

WHAT THIS MEANT TO THEM

Paul continued his exhortation on unity in Christ and living a life worthy of Christ with an appeal to what the Philippians had experienced both in their relationships with Christ and Paul. As a result of those relationships, Paul went on to outline specific behaviors that demonstrate unity and model the servant-example found in both Paul and Jesus.

At this point, the Philippians heard four parallel statements:

If there is any encouragement in Christ...

If there is any comfort from love...

If there is any participation in the Spirit...

If there is any affection and sympathy...

Bible translators generally only supply the first, *"If there is any...,"* allowing the sense of that phrase to carry through to the other three. However, the force of what Paul actually wrote is not conveyed by this method. Starting each line with the same phrase would have been powerful and driven home the point: if any, if any, if any, if any.

They would also have heard an unspoken, "Of course, there is!" behind that phrase. Paul is asking a rhetorical question. *Of course, they had been encouraged by Christ. Of course, they had been comforted by love. Of course, they had participated in the Spirit. Of course, they had known affection and sympathy.* Every listener in Philippi would have been reminded of times in their lives when each of these experiences was dynamic and vital to their relationship with Christ and each other.

THE FOUR COMMON EXPERIENCES

Encouragement in Christ

The chapter break between Philippians 1:30 and 2:1 is not as bad as some found in Scripture. However, it can still lead to disconnecting the suffering mentioned in 1:30 from the encouragement in Christ in 2:1. There would have been no such break for the Philippians as they heard the letter being read. (There were no numbers in the letter they received.) The suffering the Philippians faced in Christ had been mitigated by the encouragement they received in Christ. Each of the Philippian Christians was able to recall experiences of suffering and encouragement in Christ—if not their own, certainly those of others in their church. Yes, they had faced suffering and hardship as they believed and practiced a faith that was at odds with the culture in which they lived, but they had also received great encouragement by Christ, and emboldened to share their faith with those around them.

Comfort in Love

In the midst of not only opposition from the surrounding culture, but also the normal hardship of life in a fallen world, the Philippians felt the comfort of love. That love came, not only directly from Christ, first by way of their salvation and then in the midst of opposition as the encouragement of the first clause indicates, but it has also came from Christ's people, their fellow believers. Paul had been on the receiving end of this comfort as the Philippians had supported him spiritually with their prayers, materially with financial support, and emotionally with the sending of Epaphroditus to serve him during his imprisonment. Such comfort, born out of love, had certainly strengthened both Paul and the Philippians.

"Strengthened" is indeed the correct word to use when we speak of being comforted, especially by Jesus. The word "comfort" is a combination of two Latin words, *com* and *forte*. The word *com* simply means "with." Anyone familiar with music knows the term, *fortissimo*, which is to play with power. To "fortify" something is to strengthen it. So to comfort someone, is to bring them strength in the midst of hardship, giving that person what they need to continue to fight and press ahead. The one who brings comfort brings strength to the one who may be on the verge of being overcome by their circumstances. To comfort is not merely a soothing of pain, but an assurance of your ability to rise above the hardship and battle against it with courage.

Participation in the Spirit

The unity that comes from the work of the Holy Spirit in our lives would have been clearly evident in the congregation at Philippi. What we know of the first several converts (Lydia and her household, the jailer and his household, and the demon-possessed girl) shows enough outward diversity that it would have been an odd group to behold. The growth of the church over the intervening dozen years would only have added to that mix. Romans, Greeks, Jews, slaves, freemen, soldiers, artisans, farmers, and more, united in a love for one another that only made sense in light of the Holy Spirit binding them to one another. The participation in the Spirit is more than a common experience, but a unifying factor. They shared the reality of the indwelling of the Holy Spirit who made them one body in Christ. "Participation in the Spirit should sound the death knell to all factiousness and party spirit, for it is by this 'one Spirit' that they were all baptized into one body (1 Corinthians 12:13)" (O'Brien1991, 175).

Their participation in the Spirit would have included their expressions of love for one another, but also their time of corporate worship when the manifestations of the Holy Spirit would have been evident. Even though Paul did not go into any detail about that with the Philippians, Paul's teaching regarding the Holy Spirit's presence during worship is apparent enough in his other letters (1 Corinthians 12, 1 Corinthians 14), so it is safe to assume that the Philippians also experienced the manifestations of the Spirit, yet without the divisiveness and confusion of the Corinthian experience.

Affection and Sympathy

Affection is too tame a word to fully appreciate what the Philippians heard in Paul's words. The original language pointed to the *bowels*. In other words, this "affection" was a deep-seated, from the gut, agonizing, and yearning, born out of genuine concern for another. It is a passionate response that is motivated by love. The Philippians had been on the receiving end of that kind of mercy and compassion, first in their conversion to Christ, and later as they had walked together in His name. They had heard the story of Christ's humiliation and death as He suffered for their sake and their salvation. The telling of His crucifixion would have needed no embellishment for them. Crucifixion was something many of them had witnessed, and perhaps some of them had carried out in their duties as Roman soldiers. They would have been well aware of the yearning for them that Christ had from the very depths of His being.

They also knew that Paul had the same passion for them. His visits with them were marked by deep sympathy and compassion. His sacrifices for them, his words of love, and tenderness toward them: all reinforced their relationship, making it perfectly reasonable for Paul to bank on that relationship as he urged them to even greater unity and love for one another.

MAKE MY JOY COMPLETE!

Having reminded the Philippians of the encouragement, comfort, participation in the Spirit, and affection they had all received, Paul pointed them to the appropriate response to all of these. It was *not* to sit back and bask in the delight and joy of it all, but rather to press forward. To hearken back to the words of Jesus:

> *"To whom much was given, of him much will be required."*
> (Luke 12:48)

Since they had received such blessings since coming to faith in Christ, they had a responsibility to live worthy of the calling they had in Christ. Paul added weight to his exhortation by appealing, not only to what they had received in Christ, but also what it would mean to him if they did this. If they lived lives worthy of Christ, Paul's joy would be made complete! They were united in Christ, being of one mind, having the same love for one another, and being of one accord, Paul would be pleased. In essence, Paul was saying, *Do this for me!* He was making use of his relationship as their father in the faith and calling them to do as he asked in that capacity. In Roman culture, the *pater familias,* or father of the family, had a significance amount of authority to direct family members to do and act in specific ways. He really ruled the roost! In a spiritual sense, Paul was making that appeal, not commanding as much as urging, the Philippians to be united, so that he could have full and complete joy. "At the beginning the focus is on Christ—and what is theirs by being 'in Christ'....As Paul moves to the next two clauses, the primary focus again seems to be on the Philippians' experience of God's love and participation in the Spirit...When he reaches the fourth clause...the direction seems to shift toward their relationship with him (Paul), thus leading directly to the imperative, "complete my joy" (Fee1995, 179).

What father would not be overjoyed by seeing his children live in such harmony? For the Christian father, there is the added delight of them sharing a common cause in the spread of the gospel. For one who is facing death as Paul was, the knowledge that his children, living on after him, would do so in unity in Christ and carry on the ministry that he began among them, would be a great comfort and joy.

The practical application for the Philippians was the directive to be united in love and of one mind. Paul was not asking them to *think* the same things, but to have the *same focus and determination*, the *same direction and purpose*. It is a good thing to be united in what we believe about Jesus. However, that is simply a starting point. It would be far too easy for the Philippians to be united in a doctrinal idea, but divided in practice. Paul wanted them to be united in the direction and the determination they had in Christ too. He was setting up what will be demonstrated as being the mind of Christ in Philippians 2:5-11. The Philippians were being asked to be united in their mindset, focus, and also in their emotional connection to one another and Christ (Fee1995, 187).

To achieve this unity of mind and purpose, they were going to have to change some other aspects of their minds, failings all too common among fallen human beings. Paul had already told them about some brothers who were preaching the gospel out of their own envy and jealousy. These brothers were only concerned with the advancement of their own reputations and status. They had no thought for what Paul, a brother in Christ, was going through in prison, facing death. The

Philippians had heard about this just moments before, as the letter was being read to them. Suddenly, they are being told to do the opposite!

One can imagine what they thought when they heard of these brothers who thought only of themselves and thought nothing of Paul and his situation. They would have had some amount of disgust and sorrow over the behavior of those brothers. There was barely enough time for the echo of those words to fade away, and Paul tells them to make sure they do nothing from rivalry or self-centeredness. And Paul didn't have to point back to those brothers. He simply needed to bring up the issue of rivalry and self-centeredness. The Philippians are already primed to find such behavior abhorrent. Now they are being forced to check their own hearts and make sure that same thing is not present, even in a nascent form.

Paul does not stop with what not to do. He goes on to give them instructions on what *to do*. Their mindset, their way of looking at the world and others, was to be one in which they humbly considered the needs of others as more important than themselves. The call to humility in a Roman colony full of veteran soldiers was as countercultural as it gets. Roman and Greek culture viewed humility as a weakness, a shortcoming, a very unmanly character trait. It was shameful to be humble. (Fee1995, 188). The Philippians would have been forced to do some wrestling with this idea of humbling yourself.

What Paul is not doing is saying anything about one's self-esteem or value as someone made in the image of God. It is not that other people are of more intrinsic value than you are, but rather that when you considered your needs in comparison to those of others around you, you should put others before yourself. Verse 4 goes on to bring the balance to the equation, saying that you should look out for the needs of others with equal concern and energy, as you look to your own.

WHAT IT MEANS TO US

The theme of Christian unity can never be emphasized enough. That unity is built on a mindset of serving others at their point of need. When everyone thinks of their own needs and desires first, then life becomes a competition to get ahead, stay ahead, and keep other people from getting ahead of you. Families are not supposed to function that way. One could make the case that a contributing factor in the demise of families today stems from adults focusing on their own needs and wants at the selfish expense of other members of the family, especially their children. In fact, many young couples do not wish to have children because they know that will force them to live a servant lifestyle.

The body of Christ is often described in the Bible in family terms. Collectively, we pray to God *our* Father. We refer to Jesus as the *first-born* among His brothers and sisters. We refer to one another as brothers and sisters in Christ. This is not intended to be a religious platitude, but an *actual description* of our relationships with one another in Christ. Being family needs to extend beyond mere words. It needs to be demonstrated in action. That action means putting the needs of others in the forefront and making sacrifices to meet those needs.

> **Being family needs to extend beyond mere words.**

This also means that our sense of worth cannot, and must not, come from a psychological notion of self-esteem or worse, positive thinking. Our sense of value must be based in a theology that understands what it means to be made in the image of God, and to be so loved by God that He sent His Son to die for us (John 3:16). I am not valuable because I think I am. I am valuable because the Creator of the universe said I am. I don't need to deny my shortcomings and sin to feel valuable. I need to appreciate that God knows my sin full well—and still put my need for salvation at the top of His list, and met my need through the life, death, and resurrection of Jesus.

If that is true, then there should be nothing keeping me from setting aside my own desires for prominence and position, in order to look out for the needs of others. I lose nothing by doing so. In fact, I gain much. The Bible lifts serving others to the highest of virtues. John the Baptist came in the role of a servant, paving the way for the Messiah. John said of himself that he must decrease so that the Messiah would increase (John 3:30). Jesus said of John the Baptist that there was no one greater in the kingdom of God than John. (Matthew 11:11). John willingly humbled himself for the sake of the Messiah and the result was that Jesus honored him as the greatest. It is exactly what James points to when he writes:

Humble yourselves before the Lord, and he will exalt you.
(James 4:10)

CHAPTER 6

CHRIST'S JOY IN SACRIFICE

[5] *Have this mind among yourselves, which is yours in Christ Jesus,* [6] *who, though he was in the form of God, did not count equality with God a thing to be grasped,* [7] *but emptied himself, by taking the form of a servant, being born in the likeness of men.* [8] *And being found in human form, he humbled himself by becoming obedient to the point of death, even death on a cross.* [9] *Therefore God has highly exalted him and bestowed on him the name that is above every name,* [10] *so that at the name of Jesus every knee should bow, in heaven and on earth and under the earth,* [11] *and every tongue confess that Jesus Christ is Lord, to the glory of God the Father. (Philippians 2:5-11)*

WHAT THIS MEANT TO THEM

This is one of the most profound, beautiful, and theologically rich passages in the entire Bible. It is hard to imagine the Philippian congregation taking it all in at one sitting. The beauty of a poetic hymn is present here. It is one that has had scholars debating for ages about where the words originated and how widespread their use was in the early church. It is filled with depth concerning the very nature of Jesus as God and man. It speaks of the heart of God to have Jesus come to suffer and die for us. It points to the glory He willingly gave up in order to take on human flesh, and of the inevitable day when all the world will bend the knee before His glory, and declare Him to be Lord and Christ.

There is so much here that one of the preeminent scholars of Philippians, Ralph Martin, wrote a landmark 300+ page commentary on just these six verses in 1997! Its title, *A Hymn of Christ,* points to the belief that this passage was some type of hymn that would have been well known in the early church. Exploring all the reasons for that thinking and the nuances that surround it are beyond the scope of this work. However, based on the research, it is safe to assume that it was some type of early hymn or poem that may or may not have been written by Paul, and may or may not have been known to the Philippians before hearing it read in Paul's letter. None of that changes the content of the passage or its profound impact though.

If the Philippians had not already been given enough reason to set aside any possible division among them to maintain their unity, Paul played his trump card in these verses. He had already alluded to Christ as our example in how we deal with suffering and opposition. Now he makes it crystal clear that Jesus is the ultimate example, and if we are *in* Christ, then we will have no other course of action, but the one taken by our Lord, our model for living.

> *Have this mind among yourselves which is yours in Christ Jesus.* *(Philippians 2:5)*

Paul has already urged the Philippians to be of one mind (1:27, 2:2); now he is telling them that this mind is actually *the mind of Christ,* and the focus, intention, and purpose of Christ. Furthermore, because they are *in* Christ, it is also their focus, intention, purpose as well. The repeated emphasis on the "mind" in such a short time would not be lost on the Philippians. Paul was telling them that this had to be what characterized their approach to life. It had to be the basis of their actions because it was the basis for the actions of Christ when He came into the world.

The Philippians heard one of Paul's most repeated phrases: *in Christ*. He used this phrase so often in his letters that it ran the risk of becoming a cliché, thereby losing the impact it was intended to convey. To be *in Christ* is to be united with Him by the indwelling of the Holy Spirit. It is to have a new identity and an assurance of salvation. Having the mind of Christ is integral to being *in Christ.* Our unity with Him, the bond of the Holy Spirit, and the awareness of our salvation, should all result in possessing the *mind* of Christ.

> To be in Christ is to be united with Him by the indwelling of the Holy Spirit.

Then Paul goes on to describe the mindset Jesus had before He even came into the world through the incarnation. The power and significance of that mindset was that Jesus possessed it, even in His position *before* the incarnation. Considering that position leads one to think there was no way Jesus would come into the world to be a sacrifice because *before* His incarnation, Jesus was in the very form of God.

There has been a great deal of debate surrounding what Paul meant by the phrase "very form of God." It is crucial to understand what Paul meant and what the Philippians heard since this has had a huge impact on our understanding of the divinity of Jesus and how that relates to His humanity. The word Paul used that is translated *form* is the Greek word *morphe*. It is a familiar enough Greek word that has found its way into English nearly intact. When we speak of the transformation that a caterpillar goes through to become a butterfly we use the word "metamorphosis." It speaks of a complete change of form. The caterpillar was one thing and it became another. But it is more than simply the changing of an outward appearance. There is such a complete change that one becomes something completely other. It changes its very essence and identity. It is intrinsically different from its other form.

By using *morphe* to describe Jesus prior to the incarnation and saying that He was in the very form of God, Paul was referring to more than Jesus' appearance or outward presentation. He was saying that prior to the incarnation, Jesus shared in the very nature or essence of God. In particular, He shared God's glory (Martin1997, 105). "It offers the attractive picture of the preexisting Lord as reflecting the divine splendor as the image of God (cf. Col. 1:15) and matches exactly the thought of John 17:5: 'the glory which I had with thee before the world was'" (Martin1976, 95).

What this meant to the Philippians was that Jesus, preexisting in the *morphe* of God, was equal with God having the "essential nature, as opposed to exterior form or shape" (Martin1976, 94). Jesus was clothed in the glory of God; and in His essence, was God. He was not a super human, or a first created being, or some demi-god. He had equality with God in nature, position, and glory.

This equality with God was not something that He was compelled to cling to or grasp. Jesus could have chosen to remain in that place of glory and hold onto His place of equality with God. He could have chosen to remain on the throne of glory for His own advantage, but He did not. Moved by love and compassion, Jesus laid it all down instead. This is in stark contrast to the way human beings cling to power and glory.

The Philippians could have easily thought of a series of emperors who clung to the glory of being emperor. In their own lifetime most of the Philippians would have been familiar with up to four ruling emperors: Tiberius, Caligula, Claudius, and Nero. Tiberius came to the throne in AD 14 after Augustus was, in all probability, poisoned by his wife. Caligula gained the throne when Tiberius either died of natural causes or was assassinated by Caligula. Claudius came to the throne when a group of senators assassinated Caligula, and he lost the throne when he was killed by his wife in favor of Nero taking the throne.

Human beings vie for power and position, and along the way, destroy one another. That is the world the Philippians knew.

The contrast of Jesus is so stunning that it would have inspired awe and wonder in their hearts and minds. People did not give up glory willingly and they did terrible things to others in order to achieve it and keep it. Jesus did just the opposite (Philippians 1:7). Rather than doing all He could to keep His position, He freely let go of it and made Himself nothing, taking the form of a servant. Again, the word *morphe* is used here. Jesus did not just take on the outer appearance of a servant. He actually took on the very essence of being a servant. Just as *morphe* meant the very essence of God in verse 6 and not just an outward appearance, so here in verse 7, it means that Jesus took on the very essence of being a servant and not just the outward appearance of it. While the emperor gathered more and more servants around him to demonstrate his glory and power, Jesus gave up all the trappings of glory, the worship of the heavenly host, and became a servant of humanity!

Immediately after all this emphasis on the *morphe,* Paul threw something of a curveball at the Philippians in verse 8. The ESV says that Jesus "being found in human form humbled Himself." At this point what the Philippians heard becomes crucial. One would expect that Paul would again use *morphe,* and that it had been translated into "form" as it was in verses 6 and 7. But that is not the case. Here Paul used the word *schemati.* Think of the word schematic. A schematic is a representation of something else.

The difficulty we face in translation is that in verses 6, 7, and 8, we have not two words *but three* that are closely related, and leave us with the challenging task of distinguishing them in English. We have already seen in verse 6 that *morphe* is rightly translated as *form:* Jesus being in the *form* of God. In verse 7, once again, He takes on the form, *morphe,* of a servant. At the end of verse 7, the ESV says that Jesus was "born in the likeness of men." "Likeness" in this case is the word *homoiumati.* It is the word Paul uses in Romans 8:3 when he says Jesus came in the "likeness of sinful flesh." Then we have *schemati* in verse 8 as we have already seen.

Here are three words in close proximity to one another, all being used to give us some understanding of the nature of who Jesus is—in both His humanity and divinity. Gordon Fee helps us with the relationship between *homoiumati* in verse 7 and *schemati* in verse 8, seeing them as stating the same thing with merely a stylistic word choice on Paul's part. The two words are both getting to the same idea: "the primary sense of the word has to do not with the essential quality of something, but with its external, that which makes it recognizable" (Fee1995, 125).

So what did the Philippians hear in verses 6-8 with all this discussion of Jesus' likeness and form, and not grasping equality with God? First, Jesus in His preexistent state was, in fact, God. There was no doubt about it. He gave up that position to become an actual servant. In both these forms He possessed all the essence of being God and being a servant. It was not simply an act, or that he looked like God or a servant. When it comes to His humanity, He, in fact, did truly become human, *but there was some way in which He was not identical in essence to other humans*. That is why Paul uses the words *homoiumati* and *schemati.*

The connection to Romans 8:3 is important here. Jesus was human. He was born as a man and experienced all of what it means to be human, with one major and absolutely essential difference: Jesus did not know or experience sin as something He committed and was guilty of doing. He was free of sin (2 Corinthians 5:21, Hebrews 4:15).

The Philippians would have had a much easier time grasping the nuances of what Paul was saying than we do. They would have heard both the affirmation of the full divinity of Jesus Christ as well as the affirmation of His full humanity, yet a humanity that did not share the sinful essence that we all possess. Jesus was truly Christ and Savior, the King, not just of the empire but of the entire cosmos.

The Philippians, both Jew and Greek, would have grasped the distinction Paul was making in his use of form and likeness, *homoiumati* and *schemati*. That does not mean they would have fully understood or easily embraced the implications of God coming into the world, in the flesh, incarnate. For the Jew, the idea that the transcendent God, the Holy One, would lower Himself and become man was blasphemous in the extreme. For the Greek, gods took human form all the time, even having physical relations and siring children. But to think that such a god would become a servant, subject to human suffering would be far outside their worldview. All of this leads us to the most shocking part of this passage for the first century reader, Jew or Greek: The King of Creation was crucified like a low-life criminal of the worst possible kind.

A KING CRUCIFIED

Currently in Christianity, especially in the evangelical groups that take the Bible seriously and appreciate human sin, Jesus' role as our Savior is the focal point. Even in an increasingly post-Christian culture, there is still enough residual understanding of Christianity that people who do not follow Jesus know that He is considered the Savior of the world. When we look at Jesus on the cross, it is often through the theological lens of the Savior who suffered and died for our salvation. That is certainly biblical and true; but if that is all we see, we are in serious danger of missing something crucial that the Philippians would not have missed: It is the King of Kings who gave His life on the cross for our salvation.

Paul does not call Jesus a king in this passage, but the description of how Jesus emptied Himself and became a servant—*to the point of death* is incomplete without Paul's description of Jesus being highly exalted so that *every knee would bow and every tongue confess that*

Jesus Christ is Lord (Philippians 2:10-11). The person you bow down to and declare as Lord is the King who has authority over you. Jesus is the cosmic King who rules the universe. For a people who were ruled by an absolute monarch in the person of the Roman emperor, declaring Jesus to be the ultimate King was a shocking and provocative act, especially in light of the crucifixion.

In addition to clearly hearing that Jesus was God come in the flesh, the Philippians heard that He was also like no other king because He willingly and freely became a servant to the point of the cross. The Roman emperor demonstrated power by having an empire filled with people who bowed to his every demand and desire. The emperor demonstrated his glory in every possible way. He looked to accumulate more glory at the expense of others. Jesus was the antithesis of the emperor. The contrast could not have been more startling. The retired soldiers, the government officials, the average citizens of Rome who lived in Philippi would all have had vivid pictures in their minds of the glory of Rome contrasted with the glory of Christ. The contrast between an emperor who sought to gain more glory for himself and King Jesus, who had emptied Himself of glory, for the sake of others could not have been more stark.

> Jesus was the antithesis of the emperor.

Jesus set aside His glory in order to take on the form of a servant, but He did not *remain* in that humble state, and did not set aside His glory for all eternity. Instead, as a result of His sacrifice and love, the Father raised Him up and restored Him to His place of glory, and gave

Him a name at which every knee would one day bow, every tongue confessing that Jesus Christ is Lord to the glory of God the Father. The Philippians would have heard that the glory which is Rome would one day be surpassed by the glory of Jesus in such a way that all the world, even all creation, would bow down to Him.

As vast as the Roman Empire was—stretching from Britain in the west to the edge of Persia in the east—everyone knew there were places beyond the edge where the glory of Rome *did not* shine. The Picts in the north of Britain, what we now call Scotland, never came under Roman rule. The Persians were notorious for holding back the expanse of Rome. No matter how vast and glorious Rome seemed, there were always those who did not bend the knee to the glory of Rome. Not so with Jesus. One day *every* knee would bend to Him. The Philippians would have heard an astonishing statement of the strength and power of this crucified King, and they would have understood that His power came, not in spite of being crucified, but *because of it*.

WHAT DOES IT MEAN FOR US?

This text holds two major implications for us today. One is theological and the other is practical. The theological comes first because what we do with the theological implication determines the practical implication. Theologically the passage is as clear a statement of the humanity and divinity of Jesus as you will ever find. When correctly understood through the perspective of the first century audience, there is no other conclusion to draw but that from the earliest days following the death, resurrection, and ascension of Jesus, the first Christians understood Him to be God Incarnate. This realization led to the second implication, the practical one: their entire lives needed to be shaped and guided around their devotion to Jesus above all else, even if that meant becoming servants to the point of death.

Perhaps there is no doctrine from the Bible that needs to be more clearly and consistently taught among Christians these days than the deity of Jesus and the understanding that He is both fully God and fully man. Some might think that the gospel would be the most important doctrine to teach. I never want to be seen as downplaying the gospel, but let's not forget that if Jesus is not God Incarnate, fully God and fully man, then His death of the cross, which is at the heart of the gospel, is meaningless. If He were not God Incarnate then He was simply a man whose death would have absolutely zero saving benefit for the rest of us. He would have deserved death for His own sins and could not have been our substitute. His death would have been tragic and sad, but nothing more. He simply would have been added to the list of those tragically killed by the Romans.

Some might suggest that the resurrection is the most important doctrine because, as Paul says in 1 Corinthians 15:

> If in Christ we have hope in this life only, we are of all people most to be pitied. (1 Corinthians 15:19)

However, the point of the resurrection was that it vindicated Jesus and demonstrated *His deity and victory over death for us*.

Why do I believe this is such a crucial doctrine to get right? Let's look at the options so we can better understand this. First the teaching of Philippians 2:5-11 makes it clear that the earliest Christians understood Jesus to be both fully God and fully man. In addition and more importantly, it is clear that Jesus self-identified as being God. I won't go into detail here to prove that point. I wrote about this in *The Provocative God: Radical Things God Has Said and Done.* Additionally, far more brilliant people than I have been affirming this for 2,000 years.

With the foundation that the Bible in general and Jesus in particular both affirm that Jesus is God in the flesh, the options before us become very clear. C.S. Lewis was notable for clarifying what is at stake here with his famous "Lord, Liar, Lunatic" trilemma. Jesus claimed to be God. There are only two conclusions we can draw from that. Either He was, in fact, God or He was not. If He was not, then He was lying or crazy. There are no other choices. If I claim to be the coach of the Pittsburgh Steelers, there are only two conclusions to draw: either I am or I am not. There is no in-between.

The same is true for Jesus and His claim to deity. From that there are some other conclusions we can draw. Let's suppose we decide that Jesus is in fact *not* God. There are only two conclusions we can draw from this, either He knew He was not God and was a bold-faced liar—or He honestly *believed* He was God and was mentally deranged. Lewis puts it as only he can in *Mere Christianity*: "He would either be a lunatic — on the level with the man who says he is a poached egg — or else he would be the Devil of Hell." If Jesus knew He was not God, then He is either a liar from the pit of hell or a poached-egg crazy man. One or the other.

The common practice of treating Jesus like a great holy man, prophet, and moral teacher just doesn't work. If you think about it, you cannot have Jesus as the great moral teacher and not have Jesus God Incarnate. Why not? Because central to what He taught and what the

Bible teaches about Him is that He was God Incarnate! *Liar or lunatic are your only options if you refuse to accept Jesus Christ as fully God and fully man.* And Jesus would rather you went that direction instead of holding a position that sees Him merely as a good moral teacher.

Jesus is not big on fence-sitting (what He calls being lukewarm in Revelation 3:16). Just as you would spit out lukewarm water, Jesus spits out lukewarm people. Lukewarm people *think* they are OK with Jesus: not too serious about Him to be fanatical or have Him really impact their lives, but not hostile to Him so as to nix their chance to go to heaven. Jesus would rather you were hostile; at least that is intellectually honest. He can work with that. The apostle Paul, great persecutor of the church, is a good example. He was as hot against Jesus and His followers as you could possibly be, but Jesus got hold of him and turned him into one of His greatest spokesmen.

What about the other option? The one that says Jesus was not a liar or a lunatic? That option is that Jesus claimed to be God because He actually was God in the flesh. Left with that option, we are faced with the reality that Jesus of Nazareth, the carpenter's son, was truly God. Could this be? When we look at what Jesus actually said and did, it is the only option that makes any sense. Jesus did not toe the line about who He was. It's all right there in the Gospels. That leaves us with only one reasonable response: to fall on our knees and declare that Jesus Christ is Lord to the glory of God the Father.

The declaration that Jesus is God Incarnate means that the only reasonable thing to do is give our lives to Him completely and totally. This is the point Paul makes in Romans 12:1 when he urges a complete surrendering of our lives and our bodies, as a living sacrifice to Jesus, claiming that it is the only reasonable thing to do. He uses the Greek word *logikon* from which we get logical. If Jesus is indeed God, then the only logical, reasonable thing to do is to give yourself to Him as His follower, and to do so completely. It is what Jesus had in mind when He said that the greatest commandment is to love the Lord your God with all your heart, mind, soul, and strength (Mark 12:30). Doing this is the first practical implication.

The second practical implication has to do with how we present Jesus to the rest of the world. Theology has gotten a bad name in recent years. What was once referred to as the "queen of the sciences" has instead become highly suspect, even among Christians. For many people, in what has become a highly relativistic world, theology is just so much talk and opinions, and we can't really know what is true anyway—if such a thing as truth even exists. For many, Christian theology is seen as something that divides us or has no practical value for life and ministry. There is a decided anti-intellectual strand in much of the church today. Yet without sound theology, based in God's Word, we cannot really know God. The very meaning of theology is the study (or knowing of) God.

CHAPTER 7

THE JOY OF SALVATION

¹² Therefore, my beloved, as you have always obeyed, so now, not only as in my presence, but much more in my absence, work out your own salvation with fear and trembling, ¹³ for it is God who works in you, both to will and to work for his good pleasure. ¹⁴ Do all things without grumbling or disputing, ¹⁵ that you may be blameless and innocent, children of God without blemish in the midst of a crooked and twisted generation, among whom you shine as lights in the world, ¹⁶ holding fast to the word of life, so that in the day of Christ I may be proud that I did not run in vain or labor in vain. ¹⁷ Even if I am to be poured out as a drink offering upon the sacrificial offering of your faith, I am glad and rejoice with you all. ¹⁸ Likewise you also should be glad and rejoice with me. (Philippians 2:12–18).

WHAT THIS MEANT TO THEM

Verse 12 is one of the more controversial and misunderstood verses in the Bible. The idea that we are saved by grace through faith (Ephesians 2:8-9) is well established in Christianity. Yet Paul seems to be advocating effort on our part to gain something that elsewhere he calls a free gift. As we have done so far, we need to understand what the Philippians made of this text in order to understand what it means for us.

The first thing they would have noticed is that verse 13 is critical to the understanding of verse 12. Yes, it was imperative that the Philippians engaged in some serious effort as it related to their salvation; but at the same time, they must rest in the assurance that God was at work in them in their salvation, and that it was His pleasure to do so. It was God's pleasure to work in them for their salvation, so that they might live a life that was consistent with the salvation God had granted them. They had also just heard in chapter 1: 6 that Jesus who began a good work in them would see it brought to completion. God had not simply initiated a work with the expectation that the Philippians would complete what was needed for their salvation. Instead, He was promising to do all that was needed to insure that their salvation was brought to completion. Philippians 1:6 and 2:13 make no sense if the Philippians also had to strive to become saved or somehow work to achieve their salvation.

The Philippians did not hear: "Work, so that you can be saved!" They heard the equivalent of our expressions: "live it out" or "walk the talk." In other words, in light of being saved by Christ, work at living as people who are in fact saved. If I were to say, "the outworking of your faith should be a life that is consistent with the holiness of being in Christ," then the controversy and misunderstanding of the passage goes away. This outworking is done as a response to what God is already doing in you according to His good pleasure. The Philippians understood that Paul was calling them to obedience in Christ because of the gift of salvation they have been given. "Their obedience involved the continual translating into action the principles of the gospel that they had believed. The gospel brought them salvation—their own salvation, as Paul calls it emphatically, because it is God's free gift to them. But it needs to be worked out in the practical life in view of the approaching Day of Christ" (Bruce1983, 81).

This outworking of our faith has a primary motivation and a secondary motivation. The primary one is "because God is at work in you...for His good pleasure." Paul was reminding the Philippians that they had come as far as they had in life and in faith because God was at work in their lives. He is not like the gods of the Greeks and the Romans, who are depicted as capricious and petty, involving themselves and interfering in the lives of human beings for perverse and hidden motives of their own: jealousy and infighting among the gods. Instead, God was at work in their lives in positive ways that brought Him personal pleasure as their loving, heavenly Father. A God who gave His only Son over to the cross for the sake of humanity is not a capricious, petty god, but a God whose work in their lives could be trusted. Rather than living in disobedience to such a loving, salvation-providing God, the Philippians were instructed to live in obedience to Christ as the outworking of their faith and salvation.

The secondary motivation for the outworking of their faith is found in verse 16 and rooted in the relationship and debt they had to Paul. He urged them to live a godly life "holding fast to the word of life, so that in the day of Christ I may be proud that I did not run in vain or labor in vain" (Philippians 2:16). As their spiritual father, Paul was rightly blessed when they lived in obedience to Christ. As Paul was confronted by the very real possibility of his impending execution, he was also looking back on his legacy and what he had done for Jesus, thinking about the day when he would stand before Him. Paul wanted to be able to know that the work he did mattered, that it lasted, that it was not a waste of time and effort. Therefore, he urged the Philippians to live worthy of their calling as Christians, so that he would have the satisfaction of knowing he ran the race well. He was appealing to the relationship they had with him and the affection they held for one another as a reason for the Philippians to live the gospel.

These two motives for obedience are tied to a third. There are specific things Paul asked the Philippians to do in working out their salvation. He nearly begged them to live in unity with one another and avoid bickering and complaining amongst themselves and speaking ill of one another. This came on the heels of his call for them to have the mind of Christ and be unified. It was important for the Philippians to demonstrate this kind of unity, so the non-believers around them would see the difference in their lives and be drawn to Christ.

Again, the Philippian Christians were a decided minority in this Roman city. Because of this, they needed to be as united as possible. They could not afford to be divided. On a simply practical level, if they are divided, then those around them who did not follow Jesus could use their lack of unity as an excuse to reject the gospel. If the Philippian church was filled with discord and strife, it would have been very unappealing to Roman citizens who placed a high value on order and peace.

If however they had strong unity, they would shine as lights that showed a better way. Paul used the same word for lights in this passage, that is used for the sun, moon, and stars in the creation account in Genesis. These lights are parts of creation that do not exist for themselves, but to provide light for others. The Philippians were being reminded that they existed as lights for the non-believers. Just as Jesus had given Himself for the sake of the world and Paul had given himself for the sake of the Philippians, they were to give of themselves for the sake of those around them who did not yet know Christ. Refusing to complain and grumble and gossip about one another, but choosing to obey Christ in humility and love instead was a basic requirement to being lights to the Gentiles.

In hearing Paul call them to give themselves for the sake of others, the Philippians would have seen a clear example of that in Paul. He had given himself for them and had no regrets over it. They would have understood his reference to being poured out as a drink offering too. It was a common practice among the pagan religions of the day to pour an offering upon the altar of a god who was being worshipped. The image is one of the full contents of the cup being poured out. Nothing is held back. It all runs down to the ground and is soaked up and gone. Even if his life was poured out to the last drop upon the ground in the service of Christ and the Philippians, Paul would will still rejoice.

This rejoicing is motivated by the salvation Paul had been given, and the salvation that had come into the lives of the Philippians. Even if his life in the physical world came to an end because Paul has poured himself out for the sake of the gospel, he would rejoice. He also wanted the Philippians to rejoice with him. The real possibility of Paul being executed for the gospel would still be ringing in their ears at this point. Should his life be brought to an end for the sake of the gospel, Paul wanted the Philippians to rejoice in his salvation. Their joy, shared with Paul, would strengthen him and cause his joy to increase.

WHAT IT MEANS TO US

Ask people what they think is required to get into heaven and the answer from a vast majority of people, even large numbers of people who claim faith in Christ, will in some way revolve around being a good person. It can be expressed as pragmatically as a statement saying you need to do more good things than bad things, so that your spiritual account is not in the negative. Or it may be expressed with the simple statement that you need to be a good person. It should not surprise us that this is the case because it is the default mode of every major religion in the history of the world, *with the startling exception of Christianity*. Pick any religion and look at what it teaches about the afterlife, heaven, hell, nirvana, paradise, or whatever language is used to speak of a better existence following this earthly one, and the answer always comes down to *doing something* that achieves a better end. That is true for all of them—except biblical Christianity.

Given that reality it is understandable why so many people get tripped up over verse 12. We seem to be preconditioned to believe that we must become holier than we are, in order to have God's approval. We must become a better person in order to be worthy of whatever the blessings of the afterlife may be.

In the 1980s and 90s, there was a fierce in-house debate going on among Christians that became known as "the Lordship Debate". In simple terms, the debate was over the relationship between behavior and salvation. In an ironic twist, it was very similar to the debate between Protestants and Roman Catholics during the Reformation when the relationship between faith and works was hotly debated. The "Lordship Salvation Debate" centered around whether or not someone could truly be saved if they continued to engage in some area of unrepentant sin. In other words, could you accept Jesus as your Savior and be granted eternal life, and at some later date submit to Him as Lord. While admittedly not getting overly involved in the debate at the time, it always appeared to me that both sides of the debate were missing the point. While we are saved completely by the grace of God and this rests on no effort of our own, there must be practical progress in obedience to the things of Christ if that faith is genuine. It was only common sense!

It seemed that each side feared that the other was running the risk of distorting the gospel. On one hand, there was the fear that people would claim a faith in Christ and a place in heaven, and then continue to live as they had always lived without obedience to the things of God. On the other hand, there was a fear that we were requiring certain behavior, understood as human effort, in order to be saved. Verse 12 settles that conflict, once and for all. When you come to faith in Christ, and can thus claim to have salvation, then the necessary outcome should be a life that lives out that salvation.

If we are unsure of what this looks like, Paul gives us some practical instruction from verses 14-18, including a description of his own life of service and sacrifice for Jesus. There are four major examples in this section that are especially relevant to followers of Christ today: Paul calls for a life free from the grumbling and complaining that leads to division. He expects a tenacious commitment to the Word of God. He points to the high calling of pouring out our lives in service of the Lord and His gospel. Finally, he once again brings forward the call to joy and rejoicing, and the way we should be sharing that joy with one another.

GRUMBLING AND COMPLAINING

If grumbling and complaining was an issue in Paul's day, how much more so in the age of the Internet and social media, when you can vent freely and easily, ranting and raging from the safety of a keyboard. We live in a time when outrage and indignation seem to be virtues. Someone posts a story, that admittedly shows some behavior that a vast majority of people would find appalling; and the next thing you know, the web is filled with venom and indignation. What is amazing to me is that in the past, we would have never known about what some fourth grade teacher in a town of 500 people in North Dakota said to her students, so we would never have been outraged by it. What business is it of mine to get outraged over such an isolated incident in a place where I don't live and none of my family lives? In fact, I don't know anyone who does live there, or where exactly that is!

It would be bad enough if such grumbling was confined to the Internet, but I suspect that our river of indignation and the practice of grumbling and complaining is not easily confined to our computer screens. The Internet simply gives us a platform for our grumbling and complaining to spill out into our real world lives, where it wreaks havoc. It is true that we live in a crooked and twisted generation as Paul says. However, if we want to truly demonstrate the joy of Christ and our salvation, then our demeanor in the face of that crooked world needs to be one of gentleness and peace—of those who are above the fray.

COMMITMENT TO GOD'S WORD

Biblical literacy is at an all-time low in Western culture. The United States, in spite of the existence of the so-called Bible Belt, is no exception. There was a time when the stories of the Bible were part of the common knowledge base of our culture. For instance, you could mention the parable of the Good Samaritan, and most people knew the basics of the story and its meaning. That is no longer that case. Along with that lack of biblical knowledge comes a whole host of wrong ideas about who God is, and what He has done, not to mention what a life following Jesus should look like.

The commitment to God's Word needs to be twofold. First, it requires a commitment to studying and knowing the content of the Bible. In 2 Timothy 2, Paul says:

> Do your best to present yourself to God as one approved, a worker who has no need to be ashamed, rightly handling the word of truth. (2 Timothy 2:15)

Being committed to God's Word requires diligent work. It requires effort and discipline to make time to read and study it. Tools and resources to understand the Bible are more numerous and available today than ever before in history. Where should you start? A good study Bible with footnotes and articles that help explain the cultural background of a passage and its meaning should be the most basic tool in the hands of any Christian. Free resources on the Internet—ranging from the most basic of prepared Bible studies, to recordings of sermons, podcasts, and even seminary level classes, leave no excuse for followers of Christ who claim to want to know the Bible better. We have a lot of options.

The second requirement for a commitment to God's Word is to actually submit to what it teaches—even when that teaching runs counter to the flow of culture and the world around us, or when it conflicts with our own personal desires. It is not easy to hold to the historic teaching of the Bible on issues of marriage, gender, sexual preference, business ethics, hospitality, tithing, or a host of others issues, when everything in our culture promotes opposite ideas. It is not easy to adhere to the things we know the Bible teaches about personal conduct when our fleshly desires run in the opposite direction. Paul of all people seemed to understand this in light of what he wrote in Romans 7 about the struggles of doing and not doing the things that are in line with the Word of God.

POURING OUT OUR LIVES FOR THE GOSPEL

If there is one thing you can say about Paul, it is that he was committed. There were no half measures with him. Whether he was persecuting Christians before his encounter with Jesus on the Damascus road or he was proclaiming the gospel to everyone he met after that experience, Paul was all in. He did not view his life as worth anything if it was not given completely to the service of the gospel and Jesus Christ. He was willing to be poured out to the last drop—each and every drop viewed as an offering of love and sacrifice to Jesus.

How different is that from the way we are today! So many people seem to *want a little bit of Jesus* added to their lives. We want just enough of Jesus to make things better, help us deal with our kids, give us peace about eternity, and have a sense that we are helping others. But how many of us want *all* of Jesus? And how many of us are willing to give *our all* to Him? *We need to ask if we are willing to give our all so that others can come to faith in Christ.* Are we willing to give all we have, so that those who already know Christ can be discipled and equipped to grow into maturity, and then, pour out their lives for others too?

These questions can only be answered from one Source: Jesus. However, we must first pose the questions! As we do, Jesus will be faithful to reveal our hearts and transform us, so that we are actually living as we ought in the middle of our rapidly changing culture. It only takes a sincere question on our parts to get that process started. It's time we stepped up to the plate!

> ## How many of us are willing to give our all to Him?

SHARE YOUR JOY WITH ONE ANOTHER

Are people glad to see you coming? Or do they think, oh great, this is going to be a bummer? Your answer to those questions most likely depends on whether or not you are a person who brings joy or gloom to any situation. Think of the Winnie the Pooh stories by A. A. Milne. Tigger, the bouncing tiger, giggled his way through life, exuding joy to all, while Eeyore, the melancholy donkey, moaned and rehearsed how no one cared for him and always had gray rain clouds over his head. To the credit of Eeyore's friends, they loved and accepted him as he was, and were gracious toward him, in spite of it all. However, in real life, that is not how this usually works, and it's not that clear cut. You don't have to be a melancholy person to fail to bring joy into a room. You might just be someone who is never satisfied with things because nobody can ever live up to your standards. You might be someone who always puts others down, or finds fault in any situation because you are covering up your own insecurities. You might be a lot of things. The point is that there are numerous ways we fail to bring joy to a situation when we simply allow our own circumstances to override the joy of Christ that should be welling up in our hearts.

Joy and the lack of joy are *both* contagious. Paul wanted to share his joy with the Philippians and wanted them to share their joy with him. In a world that is increasingly rocked by violence and strife, we need to share the joy of Christ with one another too. Standing in a regular, unending flood of anger, hardship, indignation, and brokenness can weigh down the most upbeat soul. However, for the follower of Christ, the joy of our salvation should outweigh all of that. It is the joy we have in Christ that can (and does) grab the attention of those who are weighed down by the cares of the world. When we remind one another of the joy we have in Christ, the world that is watching us, will see something it needs and wants.

Remembering our salvation (and the overwhelming gift from God that it is) should naturally result in a joy that wells up from the depths of our soul, and overflows into our daily lives. Living in obedience to Christ (because of the outworking of our salvation) should be evidenced as delight, not difficulty. When you know you have been saved by God's unmerited favor, grace, and mercy, how could you not erupt with joy and share that joy with others? If that joy is never (or even rarely) evident in your life, then is it possible you have taken God's grace for granted; and as a result, lost, not your salvation, but certainly the joy of it?

CHAPTER 8

THE JOY OF FRIENDSHIP

[19] I hope in the Lord Jesus to send Timothy to you soon, so that I too may be cheered by news of you. [20] For I have no one like him, who will be genuinely concerned for your welfare. [21] For they all seek their own interests, not those of Jesus Christ. [22] But you know Timothy's proven worth, how as a son with a father he has served with me in the gospel. [23] I hope therefore to send him just as soon as I see how it will go with me, [24] and I trust in the Lord that shortly I myself will come also. [25] I have thought it necessary to send to you Epaphroditus my brother and fellow worker and fellow soldier, and your messenger and minister to my need, [26] for he has been longing for you all and has been distressed because you heard that he was ill. [27] Indeed he was ill, near to death. But God had mercy on him, and not only on him but on me also, lest I should have sorrow upon sorrow. [28] I am the more eager to send him, therefore, that you may rejoice at seeing him again and that I may be less anxious. [29] So receive him in the Lord with all joy, and honor such men, [30] for he nearly died for the work of Christ, risking his life to

complete what was lacking in your service to me. (Philippians 2:19–30)

WHAT THIS MEANT TO THEM

When Jesus wanted to let his closest disciples know how much He valued them, He told them that they were no longer just servants, but *friends* (John 15:15). Clearly friendship was a highly prized relationship, even in the first century. The pinnacle of love is to lay down your life for your friends (John 15:13). What Paul expresses in verses 19-30 is the value and indeed the joy that he found in his friendships. There are three different friendships that Paul speaks about in this passage, even though he never specifically mentions the word "friend." There are three relationships: one with Timothy, one with Epaphroditus, and one with the believers in Philippi. In reading the descriptions he supplies of each, I am certain Paul would have no problem referring to *all* of them as *dear friends*.

As people living in the Greco-Roman culture of the first century, the Philippians would have had a very clear understanding of friendship. Gilbert Meileander points out that friendship was a topic often found in ancient literature including Aristotle's *Nicomachean Ethics,* which has an entire section detailing the foundations and various aspects of friendship. While it may be true that Aristotle's categories of usefulness, pleasure, and respect for character can be starting points for building a friendship, personal affection was still considered an important aspect of friendship—even in the ancient world. Paul hints at all three of Aristotle's foundational aspects of friendship in this section, but the value he places on affection is also abundantly clear.

The Philippians listening to this letter being read at their gathering instinctively picked up on all three of Aristotle's aspects of friendship, wrapped in the blanket of affection Paul had for them. They would have seen Aristotle's usefulness that Paul so appreciated in Timothy as his protégé, in Epaphroditus who served him in his imprisonment, and in the financial gift the Philippians had sent to meet his needs. The joy that Paul expressed throughout this letter whenever he thought of the Philippians shows the pleasure he derived from their relationship. The respect of character, especially that he had for Timothy and Epaphroditus is also crystal clear in such statements as verse 20 when he says this of Timothy:

> For I have no one like him, who will be genuinely concerned for your welfare. (Philippians 2:20)

Likewise in verse 25 when speaking of Epaphroditus, Paul wrote:

> My brother and fellow worker and fellow soldier, who is also your messenger and minister to my need. (Philippians 2:25)

Clearer still are the words Paul shares about the illness Epaphroditus suffered and the impact it had on Paul:

> Indeed he was ill, near to death. But God had mercy on him, and not on only on him but on me also, lest I should have sorrow upon sorrow. (Philippians 2:27)

When the Philippians received this letter, it was delivered by Epaphroditus. Paul sent him back to Philippi for a couple of reasons. First, he had learned that the Philippians were aware of Epaphroditus's illness, so Paul sent him home to alleviate everyone's anxiety. Now they had Epaphroditus home again, and could see for themselves that he was well, and enjoy one another's friendship and fellowship again.

Paul also sent him for his own peace of mind. He was concerned about the Philippians too, and didn't want them to be needlessly worried. In returning Epaphroditus as he did, Paul was showing the sacrificial nature of his friendship toward them too—something the Philippians would have understood.

Additionally, the letter made it clear early on that Paul had some antagonists in Rome who were preaching the gospel out of envy, and not supportive of him as he awaited trial. Sending Epaphroditus left Paul with only Timothy as a trusted friend and companion. (Luke and Aristarchus had been with him in Rome, but had been sent on other assignments to various churches in the empire.) The willingness of Paul to suffer for the Philippians because of his love and affection for them, as well as his friendship with them, would have been driven home even further with the news that Paul intended to send Timothy to them in the near future:

> Therefore I hope to send him immediately, as soon as I see how things go with me. (Philippians 2:23)

Doing this would have effectively left Paul *alone under house arrest*. That meant no one would have been available to get food for him or fulfill any other need he might have had. Getting food does not refer to going to the kitchen and preparing something. It actually refers to leaving the house and getting supplies, something Paul could not do as he was confined to the house. In the ancient world, when someone was under arrest, they had to rely on family and friends to supply their basic needs. If you had no one, you ran the risk of starvation and death. Of course, Paul as a Roman citizen under house arrest was in better condition than the typical prisoner in a jail, but he was still restricted to the house.

So why would Paul send Timothy, and leave himself in such a state? He only planned to do this once he had some reliable indication of "how it will go" with him, meaning once he had some indication of the direction his trial would take. Would he be released or would he be executed? Whenever he got any news, his plan was to quickly send Timothy to Philippi with the report. Even though he would be alone at that point, the end would be in sight—one way or the other.

Through the description of Timothy that Paul sent, the Philippians knew Paul held him in great esteem and affection. Timothy was a kindred spirit with Paul. He was not self-centered, as so many others were, but was honestly concerned for Paul as well as for the Philippians. He is a servant of the gospel and served Paul like a child eagerly serving his father.

In many ways the Philippians heard a description of a man who was a kindred spirit. He was a servant who shared their same values and faith. This would not have been a surprise to them. Timothy was well known to them, and even had a hand in helping shape them. The DNA of servanthood for the sake of the gospel that was so much a part of Paul's character had naturally become a part of the character of his protégé Timothy's too. In turn, that became part of the character of the church they served. Like begets like.

As wonderful as the joy of friendship would have been for them, there was also a note of uncertainty and cause for concern that the Philippians would have noted when the letter was read. Paul's fate was still in doubt. As he had already made clear in the earlier parts of the letter, he might be executed for the cause of Christ or he might be exonerated and released. Nothing was certain either way.

Yet there was still hope and Paul seemed to think it a better than average hope that he would be released:

I hope therefore to send him just as soon as I see how it will go with me, and I trust in the Lord that shortly I myself will come also. (Philippians 2:23-24)

Paul had some cause to believe that God would have him released; and when that happened, he planned to come to Philippi as soon as possible. The Philippians would know of the outcome as soon as Paul could send Timothy with word, and Paul would follow as soon as possible.

WHAT IT MEANS TO US

Friendship today is not what it used to be. We toss around the word "friend" far too easily when describing our relationships. After all, Jesus spent *night and day* with his closest disciples, and it was only near the end of *three years* that He called them friends! With that as our model, do you think we might be too casual with our use of the term "friend"? Maybe. Why, for instance, as of this writing do I have 3,950 "friends" on social media? I know that looks like a made-up number, but it isn't. I have the screenshot to prove it. Some of you have more. I think the limit is 5,000. Others have far less. My wife has about 1/20th of the number I have, but if you think she is not as friendly as I am, you should know that she *actually knows* all her friends. Many of my "friends" are people I met when I was training pastors and leaders around the world for several years. If you looked at my friends' feeds at any given time, you could easily find posts in Egyptian, Afrikaans, Khosa, Zulu, Seswati, Bangala, Hindi, Ukrainian, Russian, Portuguese, Thai, Chinese, Spanish, and the occasional Pittsburghese. Yes, that's a real language from western Pennsylvania that uses words like "gumband" and "pop" for rubber band and soda! There are also a few hundred guys on my page who I coached when they were high school football players, as well as people who knew me as a pastor at Northland when it had 8-9,000 people in worship. Add to that, people who connected through the Provocative Christian Blog or because they read *The Provocative God* and you end up with 3,950 people. But I don't actually *know* them all! And they don't really *know* me.

Don't get me wrong. I love being able to connect with folks from around the world and from different seasons of my life. I love that I can stay connected with people who were friends long before any social media existed, but what does it say about our understanding of friendship when "friending" someone is a verb that indicates you clicked a button on your computer? Can't we also say we have people in our lives who are acquaintances? Can't we say we have people who are colleagues? Are not those also legitimate, and actually valuable, relationships? I have the impression that by making everyone our *friend*, we actually water down the depth and impact of what it means to be real friends. Incredibly, for all their access to relationships by way of technology, growing numbers of late teens and twenty-somethings are reporting extreme loneliness and a lack of real friendships.

The rising levels of anxiety, suicide, addiction, and other societal ills can be explained, at least in part, by our growing deficit in real friendships. Genesis 1 is very clear that we are made by God to be in relationships. God's very nature as one God in three persons, or the Trinity, shows that being in relationship is central to who we are as people made in God's image. When we don't have healthy friendships, we are operating on an emotional deficit that we desperately try to fill.

How do we fill the deficit? What steps can we take in the face of an increasingly mobile and fractured society to foster the kinds of biblical relationships that God intended for our wholeness? By looking at the key elements of where Paul finds joy in friendships, we can begin to see what we can (and must) do to be the people God fully intended in our relationships.

THE FOUNDATIONAL QUALITIES IN PAUL'S FRIENDSHIPS

Identity

The first few verses of this section cannot be read without seeing Jesus at the heart of it all. Paul's hope for the future and all he would like to do is founded on Jesus Christ (2:19). The focus of his life and Timothy's—unlike so many others—was to serve the Lord in the ministry of the gospel (2:21-22). On numerous occasions in his letters, Paul used the phrase "in Christ." This is shorthand for the deeply personal and intimate spiritual connection all who believe in Jesus have with Him. Being *in Christ* is the core of our identity. It is at the heart of Paul's understanding of himself. He is completely comfortable and confident in that identity.

> Being in Christ is the core of our identity.

So what makes this the starting point for the joyful friendships that Paul has with Timothy and the Philippians? Paul knows who he is. He is a follower of Jesus who is committed to the fulfillment of Christ's commission to take the gospel to all the world. He is a mentor and disciple-maker who loves Jesus and is committed to following Him. Because he is confident of who he is in Christ, he is able to be real and honest and transparent in his relationships with others. There is no faking it—no pretending, no covering up who he really is out of fear of rejection.

In much of the church today, to say nothing of the world in general, people are afraid to let others know who they really are. They have learned that if you don't live up to a certain preconceived standard—often one that is not based in Scripture, you can get the spiritual cold shoulder and *be locked out*. While we all know that other people's social media lives are somewhat manufactured and choreographed, we still find ourselves envious of others, and hope our far-less-glamorous lives don't get discovered.

We desperately crave being loved and accepted, so we create personas that actually keep people from getting to know who we really are. That in itself raises a barrier to the kinds of authentic friendships Paul had, and was so grateful for. If we could experience the unconditional love that is ours in Christ and fully appreciate the truth that we are valued, accepted, and loved by Christ, *no matter what*, then maybe we would have the confidence and freedom to engage in real friendships with others.

This is not just folksy wisdom or self-help psychology. These ideas are actually based in theological truth! When humanity fell into sin, there were two immediate repercussions. First, our relationship with God was broken. We hid from God as best we could out of shame of our nakedness. We felt exposed. It was as if God could see into our very soul (which of course He could). But the second repercussion was that we became distanced from one another as well. The break in human relationships comes on the heels of our broken relationship with God.

In order to have the kinds of relationships God designed for us with one another, we had to have a restored relationship with Him. That restored relationship brings with it a new identity. Once again, we can see ourselves as beloved children of God: sons and daughters who are in Christ, deeply loved and confident in our identity. *That, and that alone, puts us in a position to have healthy, vibrant, life-giving friendships.*

Selflessness

Paul said that everyone, other than Timothy, looked after their own interests (Philippians 2:21). Once you become more confident of your identity in Christ, it is possible to become more of a servant to Christ. Knowing who we are in Jesus opens our eyes and hearts to care about the needs of others. We have already seen in Philippians 2:3-4 that Paul urges an attitude of caring about the needs of others, instead of just being focused on ourselves. Jesus' attitude was exactly like this. He was willing to give up His glory, becoming a servant to the point of death, laying down his life for His friends. If you are insecure in who you are, it is nearly impossible to consistently be concerned about the welfare of others. Why? Because you are always thinking about yourself: How do you look? Are others being fair toward you? What are people thinking? And on it goes. That makes for a lousy friendship.

If you are secure in your relationship with Jesus, you have the emotional capacity to actually be concerned about others. According to human nature, Paul should have only been thinking about himself—and not the Philippians or Epaphroditus. His life was on the line. Yet he was deeply disturbed, even anxious, when he heard that the Philippians were worried about Epaphroditus. What did he do? He sent him back to them, potentially to his own detriment. Obviously, you cannot be a narcissist and maintain great friendships too. You have to be concerned about the other person's welfare, not just your own.

There is something almost magical that happens when you care for another person, especially if they didn't ask for your help. They will hold you in higher esteem as a result of your actions. They will want to get to know you better. In time, when you have a need, they will be led to step in and care for you. We see this with Paul and the Philippians. Paul had poured himself out to the Philippians: loved them, cared for them, been a great friend to them. When he ended up under house arrest and on trial for his life, they did all they could to serve him. They sacrificially gave so he could be cared for and supported.

Proximity

You can't have a relationship without being together at some point. Even with all the technology we have, there is no substitute for breathing the same air, staring at the same sky, breaking and giving thanks for the same bread. Paul knew the importance of being together in friendship. That is why he was sending his two friends back to the Philippians, and why he was planning to join them as soon as possible.

This is abundantly evident in the life and ministry of Jesus too. Much of His ministry and building of relationships happened in the context of a meal or simply being together. This is why hospitality is held up as a virtue in the Bible and throughout much of Christian history. The time spent together, especially in a home around a meal, borders on being the sacred. This is holy time. By being together and spending time together, allowing the conversation to flow where it will, relationships and friendships are built.

The ultimate example of the value of proximity in building friendships is the incarnation. Jesus, the second person of the Trinity, gave up his place in glory, and for a time, came and dwelt among us. John writes that Jesus came and *dwelt* among us, using the Greek word for "tabernacle" (John 1:14). The literary allusion is to the tabernacle, the portable tent that functioned as the temple, the actual *dwelling place* of God, as the people of Israel wandered in the desert following their release from slavery in Egypt. John is saying that Jesus came and tabernacled (pitched his tent), and took up residence among us. This was the beginning step to framing an invitation to intimacy that would be fulfilled in a short time when Jesus would pay for everyone's sin in order to mend the breach between man and God. Today Jesus invites all comers to *tabernacle with Him* in a safe place, and with a new identity found only *in* Him. We can be *close to Him now;* this enables us to extend the same hospitality we have received to others.

Opening our homes to invite people in (to be in *proximity* with one another) is a lost art in western society. We have become more and more isolated and afraid. Jesus calls us to be in the world *as He was* in the world. That means opening our lives to people and letting them get close enough to see Jesus in *us*. Your life cannot be a witness for Jesus, if people don't see your life, and don't see it *in multiple layers*. It is especially important that they see the world you call home.

This does two things. First, people get a clearer picture of who you are by seeing your surroundings. Second, it says to them, that you value them enough to let them into the space you call home and treat them as an honored guest. In that way, we build the relationships; and ultimately, the friendships for which we were created.

Relationship building and deep friendships are not accomplished in a one-time get together. Time and proximity have to go together. Jesus spent *three years* with His closest followers. That should tell us something about how this works. You will not get quality without also having quantity. There was a time when Baby Boomer parents wanted to have it all: kids, career, suburban gated communities, and more. In their effort to have it all they realized that time was not on their side. Parents began to justify spending more time on all their other pursuits and less time with children by inventing something called "quality time." Time with children became a quest for this quality time, as the quantity of time diminished. As a result, the depth of those relationships became shallower and shallower because *you cannot manufacture quality time*. It comes only as a *result* of quantity time together. Quality time is a myth.

Love

You cannot read Philippians without getting a sense of the great affection, Paul had for this church and the brothers he mentioned. There is a deep, heartfelt connection between them. It is the love that Christ calls us to have for one another. It is through this love that people will know we are His disciples (John 13:34-35). When we love others, we are demonstrating the most astounding quality of Christ, in that He loved us to the point of becoming a servant, even to death, on our behalf. And He did it for all, whether they were looking for Him or not!

Jesus' expression of love is the clue to what love is. Certainly there is an emotional component to love, but that is not the full story in spite of what pop-culture songs, books, and movies might try to tell us. Love is active. Real love expresses itself in its service and honoring of others. It will express itself in the way a person interacts with the beloved.

Consider these verses from the heart of 1 Corinthians 13, the famous love chapter read at countless weddings:

Love is patient and kind; love does not envy or boast; it is not arrogant or rude. It does not insist on its own way; it is not irritable or resentful; it does not rejoice at wrongdoing, but rejoices with the truth. Love bears all things, believes all things, hopes all things, endures all things. (1 Corinthians 13:4-8)

Patient and kind; free from envy, boasting, arrogance, and rudeness; not pushy, irritable or resentful; taking no pleasure in wrongs; honoring truth: these are some of the ways you know that love exists in a relationship. It sounds similar to James where he writes that if you claim to have faith but have no works that express that faith, then you have no faith at all (James 2:14-26). Likewise, if you claim to have love, but don't exhibit the kinds of things Paul outlined in 1 Corinthians 13, then you really don't have love.

Love needs an outlet. It needs an avenue of expression. Words are helpful, but actions are also necessary. What is fascinating about how love in action works, is that the more you express your love in tangible ways, the stronger that love seems to grow. Paul was willing to show his love for his friends by sacrificing for them. In turn, they were willing to do the same for him. If we are going to have real friendships that follow a biblical model, then being willing to express love for one another through a variety of means is a must.

This is especially necessary in a world that has merged any sense of affection for another person with sexual attraction. I see this in the way some people handle the biblical story of David and Jonathan. Here are two grown men: warriors and leaders of men. They are also best friends, willing to sacrifice everything for one another. They weep at their final parting, knowing it is the last time they will ever see one another. This is pure friendship. Yet some people immediately jump to the position that they were also gay lovers when there is nothing in the text or their culture to indicate this was the case. In fact, the exact opposite was true. But because we cannot wrap our minds around genuine love and affection that is free of sexual involvement, we miss the true beauty of their friendship.

Followers of Christ need to work at healthy, vibrant, deep, intimate friendships that are based on the relationship of love we have with Jesus. That is risky. It leaves open the possibility of getting hurt, being rejected, and having to deal with the messes in other people's lives.

But that is exactly what Jesus was willing to deal with—and more—in order to befriend a fallen and broken *you*.

CHAPTER 9

FINDING JOY IN RIGHTEOUSNESS

[1] Finally, my brothers, rejoice in the Lord. To write the same things to you is no trouble to me and is safe for you. [2] Look out for the dogs, look out for the evildoers, look out for those who mutilate the flesh. [3] For we are the circumcision, who worship by the Spirit of God and glory in Christ Jesus and put no confidence in the flesh— [4] though I myself have reason for confidence in the flesh also. If anyone else thinks he has reason for confidence in the flesh, I have more: [5] circumcised on the eighth day, of the people of Israel, of the tribe of Benjamin, a Hebrew of Hebrews; as to the law, a Pharisee; [6] as to zeal, a persecutor of the church; as to righteousness under the law, blameless. [7] But whatever gain I had, I counted as loss for the sake of Christ. [8] Indeed, I count everything as loss because of the surpassing worth of knowing Christ Jesus my Lord. For his sake I have suffered the loss of all things and count them as rubbish, in order that I may gain Christ [9] and be found in him, not having a righteousness of my own that comes from the law, but that which comes through faith in Christ, the righteousness from God that depends on faith— [10] that I may know him and the power of

his resurrection, and may share his sufferings, becoming like him in his death, [11] that by any means possible I may attain the resurrection from the dead. (Philippians 3:1-11)

WHAT THIS MEANT TO THEM

The key to this passage is found in verse 2 where Paul warns to beware of the dogs, look out for the evildoers, and beware of the mutilators of the flesh. Paul had warned the Philippians about these people before, and found it important to do so again. The Philippians knew of whom Paul was speaking. He was not writing about the Jews who were continuing to follow the way of Judaism, separate from any connection to Jesus. Rather, these were people who insisted that following Jesus was good and necessary, but you also had to be circumcised if you were going to be a *real* follower of Jesus. "The people against whom Gentile Christians needed to be put on their guard, and whom Paul elsewhere denounces in the same kind of unsparing terms he uses here, are those who visited Gentile churches and insisted that circumcision was an indispensable condition of their being justified in God's sight" (Bruce, 1983,104).

The people who were making this claim have come to be known as Judaizers, meaning they insisted on obedience to certain aspects of Jewish law and custom in order to be assured of salvation. The Philippians heard the passion, even the anger, in Paul's words. Calling them dogs, while shocking to our twenty-first century ears and what we think is appropriate for a Christian leader to say about someone else, was perfectly in keeping with the issue at hand. It was a common practice on the part of first century Jews to refer to Gentiles as dogs, a reference to them being "unclean" spiritually. In the ancient world, dogs were not considered lovable household pets. At best, they were utilitarian, used for hunting or protection. Otherwise, they were filthy street vermin and avoided at all costs—vicious and carrying diseases. Paul was simply turning the Judaizers own attitude back on them. They were the real dogs.

The reason Paul was so passionate about this was because the theological position the Judaizers took cut at the very heart of the gospel of grace. The Philippians had been taught and accepted the message that faith in Jesus Christ was sufficient for salvation. Paul preached the same message to the Philippians that he wrote about to the Ephesians:

> For by grace you have been saved through faith. And this is not your own doing; it is the gift of God, not a result of works, so that no one may boast. (Ephesians 2:8-9)

A message that required faith in Jesus *plus anything else* was to be rejected as an affront to the gospel. Telling the Philippians to beware or watch out for these people was Paul's way of warning them to be on their guard against them. He was saying: *Do not let them gain a hearing. They are preaching falsehood. Their way is a way that only leads to frustration, spiritual pride, and ultimately death.* Why? Because their message relied on human, physical effort in order to achieve spiritual ends—ends that only God, by His grace, can grant.

Verse 3 makes clear the juxtaposition of the gospel of grace compared to the message of the Judaizers, and it does so in three parts. First, those who had believed the gospel, as the Philippians had, were the *true circumcision*. Second, the Philippians were the ones who truly worshiped and honored God because they were led by the Holy Spirit. Third, they were *trusting in* the Spirit and not in the flesh, or human exertion. Let's examine these points a little more closely.

THE TRUE CIRCUMCISION

Circumcision was a matter of identity. In the Jewish tradition, circumcision identified you as a member of God's covenant people. The Jews did this to set themselves apart from the Gentile nations around them. As odd as it may be to us, you needed to be able to prove that you were circumcised as a Jewish male in order to be accepted in Jewish religious society. That is why Paul had Timothy circumcised in Acts 16:3. It had nothing to do with Timothy needing to be circumcised for his salvation. The Jews Timothy and Paul would be evangelizing would have known his mother was a Jew and that he should then have been circumcised. Without that, they would not have listened to the gospel message through them.

When Paul wrote that the Philippians were *the true circumcision*, he was saying that they had a true identity of belonging to Christ through the new covenant. He makes this point in Romans 2:

> But a Jew is one inwardly, and circumcision is a matter of the heart, by the Spirit, not by the letter. His praise is not from man but from God. (Romans 2:29)

The Judaizers were preaching that unless you were physically circumcised, you have no part in the people of God. You could not be identified as belonging to God. Paul was preaching that the gospel was a matter of the heart, not the flesh. It was the state of your heart that identified you with Christ. This was foreshadowed in Deuteronomy 30:

And the Lord your God will circumcise your heart and the heart of your offspring, so that you will love the Lord your God with all your heart and with all your soul, that you may live. *(Deuteronomy 30:6)*

Physical circumcision for the Jews was to be a foreshadowing of the spiritual circumcision that God would make available to all who trusted in the promised Messiah, Jesus Christ.

The matter of religious identity would have been crucial to the Philippian Christians. The religious landscape in the Roman Empire was divided between *religio* and *superstitionis.* You don't need to be a Latin scholar to see religion and superstition in those two words. Religions were legally recognized while superstitions were suspect, and considered detrimental to the order of the state. Judaism had been granted legal religious status. As long as early followers of Christ were identified as a sect, or subset of Judaism, they had some legal protection. Once they lost that legal covering they were in danger of being hounded and persecuted as a dangerous *superstitionis.*

Living as they did in a Roman colony that had extreme devotion to the emperor and the cult of emperor worship, the Philippians would have been under great pressure to be sure to identify with the legal *religionis,* Judaism. The potential for being ostracized politically, socially, and economically was very real for these Christ-followers. Paul was reminding them that, no matter what, the benefits of *religionis* might be, they didn't need it. Their identity was in Christ. They were of the true circumcision, the true group of people who were in a covenant relationship with God. Their salvation was based on that, and they dared not dishonor it by relying on the flesh.

WORSHIP IN SPIRIT

The word Paul used that we translate as "worship" is the Greek *latreuo*. It is used almost exclusively throughout the Old Testament to refer to acts of service that are connected with worship in the temple. Paul carried this over into the New Testament, especially in this context. Those who wanted to insist on circumcision for admission into the covenant family of God's people would likely also be the people who were still, at least emotionally, connected to worship in the temple in Jerusalem. Not only was Paul saying that physical circumcision were part of the old covenant, and no longer needed for salvation, but he was also saying that worship had taken a new turn under the new covenant. Worship was now directed by the Spirit of God, not the physical practices associated with circumcision or the temple.

The temple had been the place where the glory of God made itself known. This happened first in the tabernacle, a tent that was the Exodus precursor to the Jerusalem temple. Worship of God became so focused on the temple as to be almost obsessive. When Jeremiah was warning the people of Jerusalem of the coming destruction by the Babylonians, the people cried out, "The Temple of the Lord, The Temple of the Lord!" as if the mere presence of the temple was enough to defeat their enemies (Jeremiah 7:4). In a similar way, the worship of God under the new covenant does not rely on the presence of a physical temple, or any of the practices associated with it. Worship was now guided by the work and leading of the Holy Spirit. Because of that, real worship (true worship) could happen anywhere.

Not only can true worship take place anywhere, but it also has a different focus. The glory of worship was now found *in Christ*. The sacrifice of lambs in the temple at Passover reminded people of the Exodus and how God had delivered them from Egypt, but now the true unblemished Lamb had been sacrificed once and for all, delivering us from sin and death. That Lamb was Jesus. He became the focal point of all worship. He became the One to whom we declare praise, as we are led by the Spirit of God. Jesus is worshiped for who He is: God in the flesh, but also for what He has done: secured salvation for all who believe. That salvation is by grace alone, and not by human adherence to rituals, or physical actions.

TRUSTING IN THE SPIRIT FOR OUR SALVATION

At the heart of Paul's argument was the fact that the Judaizers were putting confidence in the flesh, meaning they were trusting their own ability to live righteous lives to one degree or another. They thought their work of adhering to the Law of Moses made them pleasing to God and resulted in salvation. Even if they included faith in Christ in the equation, they were still requiring some measure of human effort in order to complete the deal. In that way, they were showing confidence in the flesh. This was completely unacceptable.

Even though most of the Philippians likely came from Gentile, and not Jewish, backgrounds, they would still have been familiar with the human religious obsession with doing things to appease the gods. The

Greco-Roman religious landscape was full of temples for the numerous gods and goddesses in the pantheon of the ancient world. Many, if not most, of the Philippians had probably participated in the worship in these temples before coming to Christ, so they were at least familiar with the practice of trying to earn some favor with a deity, even if it had not been the God of the Jews in Jerusalem.

Because of their background, it would have been very easy to fall back into the practice of trying to appease God and earning favor. Paul declared, in no uncertain terms, that followers of Jesus chose not to put any confidence in such fleshly practices, but trusted the testimony of the Holy Spirit instead. If they needed to be reminded of the futility of trusting in their own ability to be righteous, Paul reminded them of his life before coming to faith in Christ.

PAUL'S REASON FOR CONFIDENCE IN THE FLESH

Because there was a Jewish community within Philippi, even the Gentiles would have been familiar with the lifestyle of a Pharisee. The size and compact nature of ancient cities like Philippi meant that everyone knew everyone's business, including the various religious practices of your neighbors. In order to show that the Judaizers were on the wrong path with their confidence in the flesh, Paul reminded the church of his own intense devotion to the Jewish laws and customs that he had practiced before coming to faith in Christ. The list is impressive even to us today. In all likelihood, it was far more impressive than anything the Judaizers could put on their religious résumés. The point was this: If Paul had discovered—and he had!—that all his zealous, over-the-top religious devotion still brought him up short in the righteousness department, what made the Judaizers think they could ever measure up?

Paul mapped out his life in great detail from his birth through his meticulous education until the time Jesus knocked him off his horse on the way to arresting (and possibly killing) more Christians in Damascus. Interestingly enough, Paul began with his pedigree from the point of his circumcision on the eighth day as was required, born into the honorable tribe of Benjamin. Paul called himself a "Hebrew of Hebrews," meaning he was fully committed to his heritage and the all-encompassing lifestyle of a faithful Jew. He had all this as a birthright. "What the Judaizers hope to achieve by Gentile circumcision is to bring them into the privileges of belonging to God's ancient people, Israel's race, Paul had been given this privilege by birth" (Fee1995, 307).

Paul didn't rest on the laurels of his birth. Instead, as he grew he became zealous for the Law of God, and in his efforts to be righteous, he became a devout, even zealous, student and teacher of the Law, to the point of becoming a Pharisee, a group renowned for their strict adherence to the Law of Moses. When a group of Jews began following Jesus, Paul said this was an affront to the Law, and his zeal increased to the point that he admits that he became a persecutor of the church. That statement alone indicates that Paul never did things by half measure. His adherence to the Law and the Jewish traditions was so deep that he had no problem putting people to death who violated it. He finishes his list by saying that by every human measure of righteousness, he was considered blameless according to the Law.

This is followed by a startling proclamation: All of that, Paul says, was useless for achieving true righteousness before God! In fact, it was worse than useless. It was all *rubbish*! It was a righteousness of his own making, and it gained him nothing. In fact, it was worse than gaining nothing. He had actually ended up with a deficit! Whatever he thought he might have gained, he now counted as loss for the sake of Christ. When you count something as a loss, it means that it put you in the red. All your efforts to achieve something were wasted, and that effort and time can never be regained. However, Paul is fine with that! Why? Because he had found true righteousness in his relationship with Christ!

This is the crux of the matter. This is the crucial distinction in this passage that the Philippians grasped immediately. Before he knew Jesus, Paul had been trying to achieve a righteousness that was characterized by perfect obedience to a set of rules. That is how we often measure righteousness: by checking off a list of behaviors and doing more right than wrong. When we are trying to please a God who is perfectly holy, we can never measure up. Paul discovered that, instead of him striving upward to become a better and better person and scale the heights of heaven to reach God, God came down in Jesus Christ and met him right where he was. As a result, Paul had discovered a new kind of righteousness. He discovered a righteousness that came from God *through faith in Jesus Christ*. What made this different was two things: the origin of that righteousness and the nature of that righteousness.

THE ORIGIN AND NATURE OF RIGHTEOUSNESS

The righteousness Paul discovered did not have its source in his fleshly efforts. He says that in Christ he was not depending on himself anymore:

Not having a righteousness of my own that comes from the law, but that which comes through faith in Christ, the righteousness from God that depends on faith. (Philippians 3:9)

The righteousness that he was striving for in the flesh was a righteousness based on performance. The righteousness that he found in Christ was a righteousness based on relationship. This is the more common biblical understanding of righteousness: living in such a way as to be in a right relationship with God. The origin of the righteousness that Paul now claimed he termed as being *from* God. It originated in God's effort, not ours. *God* did everything necessary to establish a right relationship with us, instead of us fruitlessly trying to make it work from the other way round. It is God's righteousness that makes possible our relationship with Him when we are sinners and "unrighteous." Christ fulfilled the Law: something we had always been completely unable to do. Because of our inability there could be no relationship with God *unless God intervened*.

The fact that this is a righteousness that comes by faith is a clue that it is based on a redeemed relationship, and not human attempts at holiness. If we understand faith to mean intellectual adherence to some theological doctrine and only that, we miss the point. There is nothing relational in that concept of faith. If however we understand faith in terms of trust, which is the more biblical concept, then we begin to see the relational component of righteousness. Trust is relational. You trust a person. You trust what they

> # Paul trusted Christ instead of himself.

say. You trust their motives. You trust that their actions are genuine. Paul trusted Christ instead of himself. This trust put him in a right relationship, a righteous relationship with God the Father through Jesus the Son.

A further clue that this righteousness is about a relationship is found in verse 8 when Paul says that he counts it all a worthwhile loss in comparison to "*knowing* Christ Jesus." This *knowing* is not a simple informational awareness; instead it is a deep personal connection with Jesus. There is a Greek term for knowing, *epistamai*, that has the sense of understanding information or having an awareness of something. There is another word, *ginosko,* which has a deeper more intimate sense of knowing. Paul uses *ginosko.* He has found a deeper, intimate knowledge of Jesus as a result of the righteousness that has come from God. He doesn't just know *about* Jesus, he *knows* Jesus and *wants to know Him more deeply.*

This relational understanding of righteousness does not eliminate the need for behaving in a way that is consistent with holiness and obedience to the things of God. What it does change is the motivation. The reason for obedience is to know God more intimately and have nothing in our lives that inhibits our relationship with God.

It is not uncommon for people in the Bible to be declared righteous. Abraham, Noah, Lot, King David, Job, Moses, Hezekiah, Josiah, John the Baptist, and Cornelius were all declared "righteous" in Scripture, just to name a few. If righteous means not guilty of any wrongdoing, then we have a serious problem with what the Bible says because none of these people were perfectly holy. To be sure, they all made some effort to be obedient to the things of God, and could be considered righteous, relatively speaking, but they were not blameless—*without spot or blemish*. Yet they all had a personal relationship with God that is held up as an example for us in one way or another.

Paul wanted to have a growing relationship with Jesus to the point where he understood, and even in some way, experienced the full range of life in Jesus. That included suffering with Jesus if need be. He wanted to fully live in the light of the resurrection of Christ, so that he might be assured of experiencing his own resurrection from the dead when the time came.

WHAT IT MEANS TO US

One advantage to working in a coffee shop instead of my study or office is the chance for a divine appointment. By that I refer to the seemingly serendipitous encounters you can have with people, encounters that have God's fingerprints all over them. In the beginning of writing this chapter, there were four young women sitting near me having a very fun, and sometimes profound, conversation. It was clear they were all students at the University of Central Florida just down the road. It was also clear that at least two of them were followers of Jesus and one of them was trying to figure out how Jesus fit into things. I took a moment to silently pray for the conversation, and for the Holy Spirit to be doing His thing: making Jesus known to the one girl through the testimony of her friends. At the end of that prayer, I was struck with the idea of giving them each a copy of my book, *The Provocative God*, along with a business card as a bookmark. I just happened to have a few dozen of them in my car, which was highly unusual. So I went and retrieved them, went back to my seat, and waited till they got up to leave. I gave them each a copy and they were very appreciative. What I didn't know was that they were not leaving, just moving to some couches that had opened up.

An hour or so later, one of them who clearly knew Jesus came to speak with me. Her name was Kylee. She had been skimming through the book and came to chapter 9, entitled, "I Never Knew You" which deals with Matthew 7 and Jesus separating the sheep and the goats at the judgment. She wanted to talk to me about that passage because it had always bothered her. Even though she had faith and trust in Christ and knew she was saved, she wrestled with the fact that she was not always loving, sometimes selfish, did the wrong thing at times, and so on. To sum it up, she wondered where she stood with Jesus in those moments.

I wish I could say this was the first time I had ever had this conversation with someone, but truthfully, I get this question a lot: times too numerous to count. Lots of people who have heard and received the good news of salvation by God's grace still become trapped in a performance-based Christianity, in which they are never sure if they are good enough. Fortunately Kylee and I were able to talk about her love for Jesus, and why, even as followers of Christ, we need to remind ourselves of the grace of God on a daily basis. For the moment at least, she seemed relieved to know that not being perfect did not disqualify her from heaven. She has a relationship with Christ by faith and because of that, God has declared her to be righteous.

Oftentimes people get nervous about such grace because they are afraid it will give people an excuse to sin and not try to live in obedience to the things of God. That may be true, but we cannot allow the possibility that people will abuse the grace of God as a reason to with-hold it. To do so, means to slip into the falsehood of all other religious systems that are at the core based on human efforts exerted to gain human righteousness.

The gospel of salvation by the grace of God based on the righteous-ness that comes by faith must never be abandoned or compromised. That is why Paul was so adamant about rejecting the teachings of the Judaizers. The minute our own righteousness becomes a part of the formula of our salvation, we cheapen what Jesus did on the cross. We make God's grace conditional. That serves only to dilute the power of God's love for us, and allows ego and spiritual pride to begin to slip in.

So why bother to be good? I have heard that question numerous times in response to the gospel and God's grace as well. It is based in the idea that the only reason to do what God commands is so you are not punished, and can gain eternal life. This completely misses the mo-tivation of love for Jesus. That is what drove Paul. You can sense it in his commitment to do whatever it takes in order to experience Christ more deeply in his life. Paul yearned to be more connected to Jesus, even if that connection was to experience suffer-ing for the gospel like Jesus did.

> Nothing mattered so much to Paul as knowing Jesus more intimately.

Nothing mattered so much to Paul as knowing Jesus more intimately. Everything in his life was geared to-wards that end. This begs the question: How badly do we want to be in a deeper relationship with Jesus? At times in my life that has been the driving force. At other times, not so much. I suspect that in the times when it was not so strong, I was either caught up in my own pride in my efforts to achieve or be spiritually superior, or ironically enough, I was just tired of doing the right thing because I got caught up in performance righteousness and not loving Jesus.

Performance righteousness is tiring. It wears you down because no matter how hard you try and how disciplined you are, it is simply exhausting to try to be holy in one's own power and strength. It has the wrong motivation and the wrong goal. The motivation is either fear or ego. The goal is always selfish. What will I get out of this? Paul wanted to get closer to Jesus, and he wanted God to be glorified in that. He wanted that, because more than most, he had experienced freedom from performance righteousness and never ever wanted to go back to it.

When we are willing to bask in the grace of God and live for His glory, not focusing on our own righteousness but deeply aware of our own sin instead, we will find it much easier to extend God's grace to others. I think this is crucial for the church today. Christians have rightly been accused of being both judgmental and hypocritical. Those two things often go hand-in-hand. The reason is simple. We profess a certain behavior out of our performance-driven theology. When we don't see it in others, our judgmental attitude kicks in. However, we are unable to live up to those same standards and our hypocrisy becomes glaringly evident.

How different it would be if we were willing to admit to the kinds of failures Paul admitted. He confessed his arrogance and his persecution of the church. He admits to being the chief of sinners (1 Timothy 1:15).

When we are honest about our own failings, we are in a position to give grace and mercy to others. The world needs that from the followers of Jesus. As the Scripture says:

God's kindness is meant to lead you to repentance. (Romans 2:4b)

The world could use some kindness like that from Christians.

If you are a follower of Jesus, you have been extended that amazing grace and kindness and mercy by God, and it should result in a yearning to be closer to, and more like, Jesus. It is a motivation of love which is the most powerful of all motivators. It is love that will cause someone to lay down their life for another. It is love that will cause someone to give up all their hopes and dreams for another. It is love that drives us to live for Jesus.

When you are motivated by love to live for Jesus, there is a joy in that kind of righteousness. It is not a burden to live for him. It doesn't wear you down and exhaust you because the combination of that love and joy is actually energizing.

CHAPTER 10

THE JOY IN THE RACE

¹² Not that I have already obtained this or am already perfect, but I press on to make it my own, because Christ Jesus has made me his own. ¹³ Brothers, I do not consider that I have made it my own. But one thing I do: forgetting what lies behind and straining forward to what lies ahead, ¹⁴ I press on toward the goal for the prize of the upward call of God in Christ Jesus. ¹⁵ Let those of us who are mature think this way, and if in anything you think otherwise, God will reveal that also to you. ¹⁶ Only let us hold true to what we have attained. (Philippians 3:12–16)

WHAT THIS MEANT TO THEM

At the end of the previous section, Paul yearned for a deeper relationship with Jesus and longed to share in as much of Christ's experience as he could. He had discovered that righteousness was not attainable through human obedience to the law, but that it had to come from God, and was part and parcel of a relationship of faith in God through Jesus Christ. For one who had exerted immeasurable amounts of energy throughout his life, trying to be the perfect Jew, this knowledge brought Paul great freedom and joy. But that did not mean he would simply sit back and rest. He knew that for all he had obtained through God's grace, there was so much more. He admitted that he had not yet obtained all that he yearned for in Christ. Because of that, he would be diligent in following Christ and urged the Philippians to do likewise. He had not yet laid hold of it, but he pressed on. He put the past behind him and looked, even stretched, forward, leaning into the future with all he had.

This is one of several places where Paul used athletic imagery to speak of what it takes to be a follower of Jesus. 1 Corinthians 9:26 is a case in point. There Paul referenced both running a race and training like a boxer. Paul's use of athletic imagery would have been familiar to the Philippians, even if Paul himself was not known to be particularly athletic. The Greeks had been engaging in large scale athletic competitions for 700 years before Paul wrote to the Philippians. Much as they are for us today, athletic competitions played a central role in Greek culture. Every person hearing this letter being read had vivid images of athletes training and competing for a prize.

The awarding of the prize was filled with pomp and circumstance and was considered a high honor. It was not unlike how we award medals in modern Olympic Games or trophies for a championship. British New Testament scholar F.F. Bruce describes what this was like in the Greco-Roman world: "There is a prize to be awarded, and he aims to secure it; he looks forward to hearing the president of the games call him up to his chair to receive it. On a special occasion in Rome this call might come from the emperor himself; how proudly the successful athlete would obey the summons and step up to the imperial box to accept the award!" (Bruce1983, 121).

As Paul shared his hope for his future in Christ, the picture of being awarded the prize for having run well would shift from the athletic competitions they knew so well and the awarding of the prize by the president of the games, to running the race of life for Jesus and being called up to the throne by Him and being handed the victor's crown. This is what Paul had focused on: a life of dedication to Jesus—much like those who competed in the Greek games. The Philippians would have pictured all this in their minds as they heard Paul's words. They knew that they would have to train and practice, and compete to the best of their ability. But this would not be a physical competition, even though it required living in the physical world. No, this would be a spiritual competition that manifested itself in how one lived for Jesus.

Total dedication was the image in the minds of the Philippians. Nobody won the prize with half effort. They must press ahead, reaching out for the goal. All of the effort, sweat, toil, and pain that went into training to win that prize would be well worth it. The joy of being victorious and having Jesus place that victor's wreath on their head was plenty of motivation. Even if they had never run a race and been the victor, they would all have seen the joy on the faces of those who had, and they would want that joy for themselves.

As the letter was being read, many in the congregation may have gotten inspired to press ahead as Paul was doing, and had urged them to do. However, there was a qualifier that may have caused some to think more carefully about what they were willing to do to reach the goal. In verse 15, Paul said:

Let those of us who are mature think this way, and if in anything you think otherwise, God will reveal that also to you. (Philippians 3:15)

To have the dedication necessary to press ahead and follow Jesus, no matter what, and to have the yearning that Paul had for a deeper relationship with Jesus, required a maturity that not everyone had. The Philippians would have heard two things in this verse: First, if you were mature in Christ, then this should be your attitude, no questions asked. Second, if you didn't have this attitude, and were therefore not yet mature in Christ, then be prepared for God to reveal that to you and change your attitude. In other words, every follower of Christ should be pressing on to the prize to be found in Jesus. If you were doing so now, with all diligence, then you were demonstrating what it meant to be a mature Christian. If you were not doing that, you were not as mature as you thought you were, and needed to get about the business of being more dedicated to Jesus, like an athlete who trained hard in order to win the prize.

WHAT IT MEANS TO US

The athletic images in this passage are as relevant for us today as they were for the Philippians some nineteen hundred and fifty years ago. Every four years, we see athletes taking the podium in the Olympic Games, which have their roots in the same games the Philippians knew firsthand. We hear the stories of the dedication that went into achieving that moment of victory. They are tales of sacrifice, personal and physical; of lives and careers put on hold during years of training;

of setbacks and redoubled efforts: all this is common. Then when we see the tears of joy streaming down the faces of victorious athletes, we know with certainty, that for them, it was worth every hardship and sacrifice.

The question for us is this: Are we willing to make that same kind of effort when it comes to following Jesus? Again, this is not about achieving salvation through human obedience to the law. It is about responding to who God is and what He has done for us in Christ. It is about being so overwhelmed by the love and grace of God that you will do whatever it takes to get closer to Jesus and closer to the goal of receiving the victor's laurel wreath from Him.

In high school I played football and ran track. I have continued running off-and-on for most of my life. In recent years, I ran several half marathons, a couple of triathlons, and the Marine Corps Marathon in Washington D.C. Getting out the door to take a practice run is always an effort, especially since living in Florida means that half the year the temperatures are not runner-friendly. Even so, invariably, when I do get myself in gear and go for a run, I feel great at the end. My body may be a bit beat up and exhausted, but there is a joy, a sense of accomplishment, a feeling of getting closer to the goal that I experience, even after a ten mile practice run. The exhilaration and joy that comes upon actually finishing a race is sometimes overwhelming. It makes all the miles of running in the heat and humidity worth it. The strain of the effort pales in comparison to the feeling of delight in crossing the finish line.

Our spiritual lives can easily mirror our physical training and competition. How hard do you find it at times to just "get out the door" when it comes to spending time reading your Bible, not to mention digging deeper and studying it? How often do you find an excuse for not taking the time to pray, or to sleep in and miss worshiping with the gathered community of the church? Yet, how often, when you actually discipline yourself to go ahead and open your Bible, and get quiet in prayer, or head to worship on a Sunday morning, do you find yourself encountering God in a new and fresh way that brings you joy?

We call these things "spiritual disciplines." They are not limited to what has already been mentioned. You can also include things like fasting, journaling, solitude, simplicity, fellowship, chastity, generosity, confession, meditation, and much more. On first glance, they don't sound very joy-inducing. It is like being told in track practice that we are going to run a series of 400 meter sprints. That's one lap around a quarter mile track, and it's brutal to do six or eight of those with a short catch-your-breath moment in between. Nobody enjoyed hearing that. Yet once we got started, and especially once we finished, we felt good.

In my case, those quarter-mile sprints were especially helpful training because one of my races was the 300 meter hurdles, not quite the whole way around the track, but you had the added delight of having to clear eight hurdles along the way, each one three feet tall. You didn't want to run out of gas trying to clear that last hurdle at a full sprint only ten meters before the finish line. The training of the 400 meter sprints was essential to finishing the 300 meter hurdle race well.

Now transfer that analogy to our spiritual race described here by Paul. The spiritual disciplines put us in a position to finish well, but we need to train with them. There is no substitute, no shortcut, for getting into spiritual shape to finish the race well, just as there is no shortcut for finishing a physical race well. Mature athletes, that is, ones who have experience and have applied that experience to their training, are aware of that. Likewise, mature followers of Jesus have figured out that there are no shortcuts to being able to finish the race well with Jesus.

One of the things I learned in training for a marathon was that you need a good four to six months to do it well, depending on what shape you are in the beginning. You need that long because you need time to build up the muscles, endurance, and cardio-conditioning to be able to run the 26.2 miles. The first few weeks of training might typically involve running three days a week but only doing two to three miles each day. Over time, that increases. The person who dives in and tries to run ten miles on day one of training will be almost guaranteed to not go out and run on day two or three.

Spiritual disciplines for the race with Jesus are no different. You can't all of a sudden decide you are going to read your Bible for three hours today and pray for an hour and fast for the next seven days. You will fail, get discouraged, and set *all* those things aside. Laying out a plan, just like a marathon training plan, should involve starting slow and small, and increasing the time and the number of things you are trying to do over time. The result is far more likely to be real success in running the race we call following Jesus, and the experience will be far more joyful too. Starting slow and small will help you grow and be more consistent in pressing toward the goal.

CHAPTER 11

THE JOY OF CHRIST'S RETURN

^{17} Brethren, join in imitating me, and keep your eyes on those who walk according to the example you have in us. ^{18} For many, of whom I have often told you and now tell you even with tears, walk as enemies of the cross of Christ. ^{19} Their end is destruction, their god is their belly, and they glory in their shame, with minds set on earthly things. ^{20} But our citizenship is in heaven, and from it we await a Savior, the Lord Jesus Christ, ^{21} who will transform our lowly body to be like his glorious body, by the power that enables him even to subject all things to himself. (Philippians 3:17-21)

WHAT THIS MEANT TO THEM

There is a thread running through this short letter concerning the existence of people who claimed to serve the gospel, but did so for reasons that were less than honorable. Paul mentioned ministers who were preaching out of envy, and a base desire to somehow make Paul's life more miserable (Philippians 1:15-17). There were the Judaizers, bent on proclaiming a gospel that Paul deplored as not the true gospel at all, because they added human requirements to God's grace (Philippians 3:2). There were those who had abandoned Paul in his time of imprisonment, so that he had very few faithful people left with him (Philippians 2:20). Paul warned the Philippians not to be taken in by such people. Now he gives them a straightforward command on what to do instead. They are to follow and imitate *his example* and anyone else's who was modeling a life fully dedicated to Jesus.

The Philippians knew the pattern of Paul's life and had seen that pattern repeated in the people who were part of his team. That pattern included a life of sacrifice for the sake of the gospel and for the well-being of others. "At issue throughout is living the cruciform existence, discipleship marked by the cross and evidence of suffering on behalf of Christ" (Fee, 363). There was no more vivid demonstration of that for the Philippians than when Paul and Silas were beaten and thrown in prison in the early days of their church (Acts 16:25-40). That very same jailer who was responsible for keeping Paul and Silas in prison and possibly beating them, who came to faith in Christ when God burst open the prison doors by sending an earthquake, was probably present and listening as the letter was read!

> Look to the lives of people who demonstrate a godly maturity and do what they do.

Imitation of one's teacher was part and parcel of discipleship. Paul was giving them a reminder of what they already knew, saying, *Look to the lives of people who demonstrate a godly maturity and do what they do.* Paul repeated this in other parts of his writings too, especially in 1 Corinthians 11:1 and 1 Thessalonians 1:6 in particular. We can safely assume that this was an idea the Philippians had heard before. As Paul said earlier: to repeat the same things again was good for them and for him.

However, following Paul and other godly examples was not the end goal. Philippians 2:1-11 holds up Christ as the ultimate model and example that we are to follow. The exhortation to follow Paul was simply a means to the end of becoming *like Jesus* in all ways. Not having Jesus physically present for the Philippians meant that they needed to look to other examples to imitate. They would not have understood this as Paul glorifying himself. They knew him too well to reach that conclusion.

If there was any doubt about Paul's heart in this, it is completely removed by Philippians 3:18-19. Paul's tears are genuine. He is deeply grieved over these people. Their selfish example was a poor model for others, and led people away from living for Jesus. Paul grieved not only for those being led astray, but also for those choosing this lifestyle in the first place. There is no gloating over the destruction that awaited such people. Paul's heart ached for them: They were not only lost, but also misrepresenting what it meant to follow Jesus, causing harm to God's mission and dishonoring Jesus.

As Paul reflected on the ultimate state of these false teachers, he also thought about the ultimate state of those who chose a better path: to love and live for Jesus. The contrast between the two groups did not focus only on where they ended up in eternity, but also where they were in the here and now. In this life, false teachers were focused on earthly things. Their god was their belly, and their minds were set on earthly things. It wasn't just that they were physically on the earth (like we all are). They were emotionally tied to their life in the here and now. Heavenly things were *not* on their minds. Paul doesn't say it, but the implication, in contrast to the Philippians, is that false teachers are citizens of this world, and thus their allegiance is to the things the world offers.

The Philippians were being reminded that their citizenship was in heaven. This was a shocking statement to make to the citizens of Philippi. In their time, there was no higher citizenship than to be a Roman citizen. It had been Paul's Roman citizenship that had gained him a deep apology from the Philippian city officials, and amazement from the jailer. It was Paul's Roman citizenship that had made it possible for him to have his case heard personally by Caesar. Yet here is Paul reminding them that citizenship in this world, even Roman citizenship, was nothing compared to the citizenship they had in heaven through faith in Jesus Christ.

That led Paul to marvel at the coming day when they would experience the fulfillment of that citizenship, and be taken home with Jesus. He was not writing about when their individual lives would end and they went to be with Jesus either. Instead Paul referred to the return of Christ when He would gather all His citizens into one triumphant parade of victory when all things would be finally subjected to His lordship (Philippians 3:20-21).

The Philippians lived in a Roman city that was part of the mightiest empire ever. Rome ruled over a land that went from the borders of Scotland, through Spain and Portugal, across North Africa to Egypt and Palestine, and north through Asia Minor into Europe proper. The entire Mediterranean Sea was their own private lake! There was nothing the

Philippians knew that rivalled the glory of Rome, and the privilege of being a Roman citizen. Yet here was Paul telling them that a focus on earthly citizenship and privilege was *nothing* compared to the glory of being a citizen of heaven and the triumph that would be theirs because of their *heavenly* citizenship at the return of Christ.

Roman citizens were familiar with the idea of a triumphal parade. It was common practice for a conquering general to return to Rome and have a "triumph": their term for a ticker tape victory parade. The whole city would anticipate the day and turn out with one voice to praise the returning hero. That is exactly what Paul looked forward to at the return of Christ, and he was calling the Philippians to set their minds on that as well. Although Paul was willing to live his life in this physical realm, still tainted by sin, he longed for the return of Christ: when all things would be made right, and Jesus honored as the King of Kings and Lord of Lords.

It is at that time that followers of Jesus will see their bodies transformed into bodies fit for dwelling in a combined new heaven and new earth. The Philippians understood this as a repudiation of Plato's Gnostic philosophy that the spiritual is good and the physical was bad. If Jesus was returning as a triumphant hero and would transform the world into a new one, then the physical would actually continue. It would not be eradicated at all! Jesus was returning as the risen Christ, who had risen *bodily*, and not just spiritually, from the grave. The bodies of His people would be transformed to match His own—physically and spiritually.

Paul's anticipation for the return of Christ was infectious to the Philippians. Their experience of triumphal parades, and the joy and excitement surrounding them would have filled them tenfold. As they thought about Jesus' return and the eventual fulfillment of their mission on earth as citizens of heaven, they were gripped with joy. They were a minority, often viewed with suspicion by their neighbors and the Roman officials. They bordered on being outcasts in their own city at times, so nothing in their current situation was so wonderful that it could possibly compete with the joy of seeing Christ return triumphantly and take up His throne.

In this passage, Paul directed them as to where to set their hope, simultaneously outlining the very real dangers that they had to be vigilant against. No matter what, their hearts should be set on their future in Christ, and their feet on the path Paul had modelled for them. In the end, Jesus, as Lord, would make it right.

WHAT IT MEANS TO US

The world is full of people who are preaching the gospel for their own gain, and they have armies of people following them and trying to be just like them. Things have not changed much in 1900+ years. I read about pastors wearing $3,000 sneakers while they preached, in an effort to be relevant, or living in 9,000 square foot houses so they can relax away from the stress of ministry, or needing fifty *million* dollar private jets, so they can pray in peace! I wonder what Paul, not to mention Jesus, would say about such things! The phrase, "their god is their belly" certainly comes to mind.

Even as I write this, I can hear the push back. Aren't you being judgmental? Who are you to say where their heart is? While I can't say where their heart is, I can certainly make a judgment about the impact such things have on the witness of the church and the gospel. When people outside the faith see this, it gives them every excuse to reject the gospel message because the messengers seem to have little resemblance to Jesus, who famously had "no place to lay his head," or even to Paul who suffered shipwreck, hunger, imprisonment, beatings, and more for the cause of Christ.

My time training pastors in Africa, Asia, and South America was often spent dealing with the damage the prosperity gospel has done to a budding and growing Christianity. Obviously, there are people starting churches as an easy way to get money. Preach a message that says: *If you give to me, God will bless you*, and desperate people will line up to give their last shilling. It is their version of playing the lottery, but worse, because they are led to believe that *God promised* to reward them *financially*. And these people are desperate. They live not knowing where their daily bread is going to come from; and along comes a preacher, claiming that God wants to reward them with material abundance *if they just have enough faith* to believe it. Of course, the proof of that faith, *so that God knows you are sincere*, is to give money to that preacher's ministry. The only one getting rich in that scheme is the preacher, and not because God is blessing him (or her). These preachers are shearing the sheep.

This is not just a matter of people being a few degrees off to the left in their theology either. A little tweaking will not have them back on track. Paul wrote that they are "enemies" of Christ. They are 180 degrees off target and actually leading people *away* from Jesus. They are leading people to trust in a god who does not exist, a god who cares only about their financial success and material well-being, and has put in place a magical transaction, whereby the more you give to the preacher, the more you get back from this false god. This is why Paul was so distraught over what was happening: the very nature of the gospel was at risk.

But lest we excuse ourselves too quickly because we are not wearing $3,000 shoes and don't fly around in our private Gulfstream, we do need to ask the question: Is our belly our god? In other words, how tied are we to the things of this world? How enamored are we with the comforts of this life? How willing are we to suffer loss for the sake of the gospel and the glory of Jesus? I recently mentioned in a sermon that everyone admires Mother Theresa, but nobody wants to actually *be* Mother Theresa. How odd is that? When I was a kid and admired an athlete, *I wanted to be just like that athlete*. Somehow we can admire someone who sacrifices the comforts of the material world for others and for Jesus, but also be very certain we don't want to do that ourselves. Paul says we should *actually try* to be like these people.

If we are going to model our lives after anyone, it should be after those who demonstrate the self-sacrificing, humble nature we see in Jesus, and Paul, and so many other faithful messengers of God's grace. This requires looking for people as role models who are more in love with Jesus and His return than they are with the things of this world. The phrase in verse 19 is the key to all this: "minds set on earthly things." We should not be modeling our behavior on those with their focus on this life, but rather on people who, by implication, have their minds set on heavenly things.

Those heavenly things include the triumphal return of Jesus when heaven and earth are made one. Paul longed for the return of Jesus and most first century followers did likewise. Think of the closing words to Revelation in which the cry of the church is described: Maranatha! Come quickly, Lord Jesus! (Revelation 22:20).

Today unfortunately, most Christians view the return of Christ with fear and trepidation. Our focus is bent on trying to figure out if the return of Jesus will be before, during, or after a period of great tribulation and persecution. A whole cottage industry of fear-mongers exists that even tries to get Christians to prepare shelters and supplies to hide away, so they are protected during that time. I get the impression that people are actually afraid that Jesus might return in their lifetime. Could that be because we do not have our minds set on the things above?

To be a follower of Christ means to hold loosely to the things of this world. There is nothing wrong with having a decent house, or a nice car, or even a healthy investment portfolio. But where is your heart? Paul's heart was with Jesus, and what he wanted more than anything was to be with Jesus, and for others to know and love Jesus too. Because that was his highest priority, everything else took a back seat. Everything in Paul's life was organized and prioritized around the goal of bringing glory to God through a life that both demonstrated and proclaimed the gospel.

> To be a follower of Christ means to hold loosely to the things of this world.

A WORD ABOUT DISCIPLESHIP

Paul's insistence that the Philippians (and by extension all of us) follow his example, might seem arrogant in a culture like ours that both prides itself on individuality and is suspicious of leaders who insist on being followed. We have seen too many examples of leaders, whose faults and failings, were prominent and harmful. How could we follow a human being as Paul suggests? Shouldn't we just follow Jesus and cut out the human middle man instead? That sounds wonderful to our independent-minded twenty-first century ears, but it was not the plan Jesus gave. His plan called for generation upon generation of people who would faithfully followed Him, as they walked in the footsteps of those before them who did the same.

The very nature of what Jesus did with a small band of disciples, commissioning them to take His message to all the world, making even more disciples, requires that we follow the example of those who preceded us. The business world figured this out, as did the military. Both learned the necessity of mentoring the next generation of leaders. Jesus called for the same thing. We call it *discipleship*.

In our passage, Paul calls on the Philippians to find good leaders to follow, so they can grow in Christ and become like them. What he does not say explicitly (but they would have understood) was that this meant they needed to become the kind of Christ-followers who others would regard as role models. This process of imitating others was supposed to continue to yet another group, and on down the line—all the way to you and me at the beginning of the twenty-first century.

More than just being a role model in the hope that someone will see and follow, a disciple-making role model requires intentionally inviting people into the process and being that example. The Philippians saw how Paul did this with Silas, Luke, Timothy, and even Epaphroditus. It was what Jesus did with Peter, James, John, and the rest. The Philippians were being invited into a disciple-making relationship and were expected to pass that on. So are we. Paul refers to this in 2 Timothy 2:2 when he urges Timothy to take what Paul had shown him, and pass it on to other faithful men who would in turn replicate it with others. Those four generations of disciple-making had become the measuring stick for a multiplying ministry of discipleship. This was never intended to be a process employed only by apostles or pastors, but it was expected of *all* followers of Christ.

CHAPTER 12

THE CONTINUATION OF JOY

[1] *Therefore, my brothers, whom I love and long for, my joy and crown, stand firm thus in the Lord, my beloved.* [2] *I entreat Euodia and I entreat Syntyche to agree in the Lord.* [3] *Yes, I ask you also, true companion, help these women, who have labored side by side in the gospel together with Clement and the rest of my fellow workers, whose names are in the book of life.* [4] *Rejoice in the Lord always; again I will say, rejoice.* [5] *Let your reasonableness be known to everyone. The Lord is at hand;* [6] *do not be anxious about anything, but in everything by prayer and supplication with thanksgiving let your requests be made known to God.* [7] *And the peace of God, which surpasses all understanding, will guard your hearts and your minds in Christ Jesus.* [8] *Finally, brothers, whatever is true, whatever is honorable, whatever is just, whatever is pure, whatever is lovely, whatever is commendable, if there is any excellence, if there is anything worthy of praise, think about these things.* [9] *What you have learned and received and heard and seen in me–practice these things, and the God of peace will be with you. (Philippians 4:1-9)*

WHAT THIS MEANT TO THEM

Imagine yourself sitting in church, listening to a sermon being preached, when suddenly you hear your name called out! Not only that, but you also hear the name of another church member! It is someone with whom you have been having a sharp disagreement, for which there seems to be no resolution in sight. Everyone in the church knows it, but nobody is doing anything about it, until that preacher mentions you both out loud in public! You are both urged to get your problems settled, for the sake of the gospel and the ministry of the church. You can't just ignore this and move on, as the preacher also calls out the name of still another leader, instructing them to get the two of you together and fix this thing. That is what happened in the very beginning of chapter 4 when Paul mentioned Euodia and Syntyche by name, asking that another companion in the ministry of the gospel get involved.

Paul made this request, a demand actually, right after he called the church to set their hearts on heavenly, not earthly, things. Paul connects the need for unity to what he has just said about the return of Christ and people whose god is their belly, and whose minds are only on earthly things. The opening word of the chapter is "therefore": Paul's common method of connecting one point to another. He had just been talking about focusing on Jesus and living properly as they awaited Jesus' return. Then he says "therefore", which means "because of that truth." Because of what he had just said, these two women needed to become united once again for the cause of Christ. Christian unity was so important, especially for this minority community, that Paul was willing to call them out publicly, thus engaging the whole church, not just his unnamed trusted companion, to rectify the situation.

This seems harsh to us, but it would not have felt that way to the Philippians. Paul has reminded them of the great affection he has for them, meaning *everyone* in the church at Philippi. They are his "joy and crown": Those words are consistent with the whole tone of the letter, from the very beginning when he let them know of his love for them and how often he thought of them and prayed for them. In fact, it is because of how deeply he cared for them that he urged them now to take whatever steps are necessary to maintain the unity of the body. Paul further softened the blow for these women (and the entire church) when he reminded everyone of how important both of them have been to him in ministry. These two women were fellow partners in the ministry. However, in order for that ministry to continue, they had to restore unity. Even the slightest division in the body opened the possibility for that ministry to be hijacked and damaged. Mentioning that their names were written in the Book of Life would have reminded them of what was at stake.

Not only is unity on Paul's mind. There is another thread throughout this letter. He is also concerned that the Philippians remain faithful to the cause of Christ. This is connected to what he just said about the return of Christ. In light of the fact that Jesus would one day return triumphantly and establish His kingdom for all time, they needed to stand fast. They needed to remain faithful to the gospel and not waver. That meant not giving in to the Judaizers, or succumbing to false preachers, or failing to embrace the suffering that was sure to come to all who faithfully followed Jesus in a world opposed to the gospel.

REJOICE ALWAYS!

What follows is a series of quick statements (exhortations actually) that, if followed, will allow joy to continue to flourish in their church. Verse 4 could easily be the thesis statement for the whole letter: "Rejoice in the Lord always, and again I say rejoice!" Paul is not saying that the Philippians needed to be happy-clappy about everything that happened to them. Instead he was saying that, because of their faith in the Lord and their position in Christ, they always had reason to rejoice. By repeating himself, Paul was highlighting the importance of this command. And it is a command. The Philippians were to obey this through their determination to find reasons to rejoice because of their relationship with Christ—in all situations.

No matter what is going on around them—famine, persecution, illness, imprisonment, even death—they had the ability (and every reason to) rejoice in the Lord. This required a kingdom perspective that was focused on the things of Jesus, their salvation, and the eventual establishment of Christ's kingdom here. Being "in the Lord" or "in Christ" is all about being *connected* to Jesus. Their position was *in Christ,* and from that perspective, everything could be viewed differently. They could always find joy, no matter what their circumstances. The gospel and the promise of resurrection to new life in Christ does that.

HAVE A WELL-KNOWN GENTLE SPIRIT

Because the Lord is near, the demeanor of the Philippians needed to be one of gentleness. This was not something that was highly prized in Roman culture, especially not in a Roman colony that contained an incredibly high percentage of retired solders from the Roman legions. Projecting strength was what got respect. Yet Paul urged them to be countercultural to the point that everyone knew them for their *gentleness*.

The reminder to be this way because the Lord was near could be taken two ways. One could be referring back to the promise of Christ's return, in which case they hear Paul saying, *Be ready and live right because you never know when Jesus will come back.* While it is tempting to take it this way (and it is certainly not a faulty idea), I have a hunch that Paul was talking about the Lord being near each of them at all times. Because of that nearness, there was no need to be harsh, angry, argumentative, or boasting. Again, the message is about being confident in your identity in Christ. Because of Jesus, you can be a different person—one whom others will find intriguing, one to whom others will be drawn. Paul wanted the gentle and reasonable spirit of the Philippians to be known to all men. It was to be a vital quality in their witness to the world.

DO NOT BE ANXIOUS, EVER, INSTEAD PRAY

The Philippians had lots of reasons to be anxious. Aside from the regular hardships of life in the Roman Empire in the first century, they were a minority and were regarded with mistrust and skepticism by the Roman citizens around them. Their allegiance to the emperor would have been tested; any failure to honor him could have been met with persecution, and possibly, death. After all, they were reading a letter from a man on trial for his life because of his faith—the faith they shared.

The anxiety Paul wrote about comes on us when we feel we have no control, when situations overtake and overwhelm us. There is a fear of the unknown, of some undesirable outcome ahead or of not the outcome we think we need. The answer for the Philippians was to remember that God was always at hand. Reminders that Nero was emperor were placed all over Philippi. He was the one in control, and deserved to be worshiped as a god because of that. He was in control of Paul's life and seemingly in control of theirs as well. Paul reminded the Philippians God was really the One who was in control. Any concerns they had should be brought to Him with the full assurance and knowledge that He was in charge and could be trusted to take care of them, granting them His peace.

Everything—no matter how small—was to be put in the hands of God who was near. The Philippians were familiar with making offerings to the various gods in their culture, and the capricious nature of those gods. They knew there were no guarantees that requests were ever answered by these self-serving gods, so their anxiety was never alleviated by them. Even bringing one's petition to the emperor was no guarantee that their requests would be answered, and their fears and anxieties removed. However, through Jesus Christ they could be confident they were *loved* by God. Here was a God, who instead of being far off and hidden, was near to them. This God was the true God. He responded.

The assurance of God's presence and care is what brings peace of mind and a calm heart. Yet it is more than that. It is in Christ Jesus, in relationship with Christ, that real peace comes. It is not simply because of *belief* in Christ. Peace came from the new life the Philippians had in Christ.

FOCUS ON THE GOOD AND BEAUTIFUL AND HONORABLE

Paul announced that his letter was coming to a close and provided a bookend to its beginning. In Philippians 1 Paul had written:

So that you may approve what is excellent, and so be pure and blameless for the day of Christ. (Philippians 1:10)

From the beginning, Paul called on the Philippians to live in a way that was attractive. Now he expanded on the qualities of excellence and purity and blamelessness, and called for a life focused on honor and beauty and goodness. According to the teachings of their great men, such qualities were highly valued in Greek culture, so Paul called the Philippians to excel in them. Paul was aware of the respect the Philippian culture had for the writings of Aristotle and his disciples as well as Cicero and others like him. He also understood that they were a minority community being called to live a moral life in the midst of an immoral culture. Perhaps they expected to be urged to withdraw and live completely separate from their culture. Anything that appeared to be at all sympathetic to, or in agreement with, that culture might have been viewed as compromise, or leading to it. But Paul, following the wisdom of the Lord, had a better plan.

By calling them to establish qualities that were also valued in their culture, Paul accomplished two things at once: He let the Philippians know that not everything in Philippi was evil or to be avoided. Qualities like beauty and honor and goodness could be found, even in pagan culture. Choosing them was consistent with being a follower of Christ. And second, he directed them to redeem their own ideals in a way that honored Jesus. Following the example of godly people like Paul did not require that one be completely isolated from culture. Instead, the qualities that were held in common by both pagan and Christian cultures were ones which followers of Jesus should also excel. They should lead the way for their culture, not withdraw from it.

WHAT IT MEANS TO US

The Priority of Unity

Maintaining the unity of the church is of utmost importance. The conflict between Euodia and Syntyche was of such a concern that Paul called them out publicly, urging others in the church to work to bring reconciliation between the two women. Being the outcast minority that they were in Philippi made unity crucial for their survival. In the past, that was not so much an issue for the church in Western society. However, being in the majority had a negative impact in that regard. Christians were far *too willing* to be divided. As the church in the West becomes more and more marginalized, often because of our own poor behavior, unity must become a higher priority.

However, it is not just the current reality that should motivate unity. It is the prayer of Jesus in John 17, in which He prayed desperately that we would be one even as He and His Father are one, that should be motivation enough. Additionally, Paul's letters to the Corinthians are filled with a call to unity from a theological perspective. We are one body under the headship of Jesus. That statement is true of any particular local church, but also of all churches and all followers of Jesus worldwide.

Unity does not mean uniformity. It is possible to disagree about things and yet be united in our love and respect for one another and for Christ. Problems arise when disagreements become the occasion for mistrust, personal attacks, gossip, and innuendo. That leads to people digging their heels in over an issue, and not allowing themselves to continue to learn from that other person or admitting any responsibility for how things have gone so wrong.

Unity does not mean uniformity.

When things do go wrong in a relationship or disunity breaks out in a church, we need to understand that the ministry of the gospel is at stake. Euodia and Syntyche were partners in the spread of the gospel. Their relational breakdown inhibited that work. When people see Christians at odds with one another, it results in a church division. It also gives people outside the church a good excuse for not following Christ. After all, *if they cannot get along with one another, why should I be a part of that group?*

Nobody likes to be part of something that is filled with discord, fighting, and name-calling. Kids show us the truth of this. If you want to know which family in a neighborhood is filled with love and respect for one another, just look at where the kids of the neighborhood hang out. They will not be meeting in a house filled with tension. The same is true for the family called the church. Nobody wants to be part of a church that is filled with tension or heated arguments either.

When division and disunity comes, they cannot be ignored. The dysfunctional habit of covering over issues and not dealing with them appropriately only causes worse problems in the future. Paul's request that another get involved in trying to resolve the conflict between the two women is consistent with Jesus' instructions in Matthew 18. Jesus called for a three-step process of escalating involvement. Step one would have been for the two women to reconcile. When that failed, step two was for a couple of others to step in and mediate the problem. (Paul seems to be at step two.) If things still didn't get resolved, Jesus said the issue needed to be dealt with by the church as a whole. This escalating process emphasizes the vital importance Jesus placed on unity in the church.

Not only do we need to strive for unity within the local church, but individual churches need to find ways to respect one another and serve the community together. I have the amazing privilege of serving in a community where churches and pastors do just that. The pastors regularly get together to pray with, and for, one another or just have breakfast and catch up on life. The churches work together to serve the community and have an annual thanksgiving worship service together. I wish I could say that was normal in communities, but sadly, pastors are also subject to jealousy and envy and hurt feelings. I love the fact that the pastors in our community are supportive of one another and have a kingdom first mindset.

The High Value of Women for Paul

Today there are two basic positions when it comes to the role of women in ministry. There is the egalitarian position which says that men and women are able to perform all the same functions, roles, and offices in the church. Then there is the complementarian position that says that men and women are of equal value, but in some cases, have distinct roles (or offices) within the church. This usually focuses on roles like preaching and teaching, and offices like pastor or elder. In the arguments over the two positions, Paul is often accused of being oppressive towards women, even being a sexist and a misogynist.

Without getting into the details of these two positions, there is something we can say about the high esteem in which Paul held women, which gives us all an opportunity to check our own attitudes. Paul referred to Euodia and Syntyche as women who labored side by side with him in the ministry of the gospel. These women were partners with Paul in ministry in the same way that men like Clement were. Their partnership was significant, and it was respected and valued by Paul.

Churches and individual Christians need to make a special effort to recognize and encourage the contribution of women to the ministry, and that includes key roles in leadership. No matter which of the two previously mentioned positions we might hold, there needs to be greater effort in including women in leadership and as partners in the gospel. Far too often people (in both camps) only give lip service to women in leadership. Even those who allow women in the roles of pastors or elders or similar offices, often ignore their contributions, and fail to give them the respect their office and gifts deserve.

Living an Attractive Life

There is plenty of ugliness in the world today. With seemingly endless numbers of news channels, Internet feeds, and a 24/7 flood of reports from around the world, it seems that the ugliness is getting worse, and is inescapable. Whether or not it is getting worse, at the very least, we hear more now. We hear about things we never would have known about before; and in some ways, ignorance is bliss, especially when the media in particular, and people in general, seem more enthralled with the ugly side of life than with the beautiful side.

As depressing as it all may seem, there is a very large and glorious silver lining in this for followers of Christ. The uglier the world appears, the uglier people are to one another, the more even the slightest bit of goodness and beauty on the part of Christians will stand out and be attractive. As the world bemoans the pain and suffering of life, and people complain about the dishonesty of politicians, or the greed of Wall Street, or become obsessed with movies and television that glorify hatred and brutality, Christians have an amazing opportunity.

Followers of Jesus have the opportunity to paint a better picture of life by living in a way that focuses on things that are beautiful, and honorable, and lovely, and joyful. What might this look like? It could be of Christians sacrificially serving the oppressed and outcast. It could be one of Christians who approach politics and business with honesty and integrity, respecting the value of people above power and profit. There are countless variations, but overall, it is a picture of people who are willing to serve others as Christ has served us.

In a world full of hate, that is a picture that those around us will heed. The goodness of the Lord is what they are really looking for. We have a lifetime in which to reflect that.

CHAPTER 13

THE JOY OF CONTENTMENT

¹⁰ I rejoiced in the Lord greatly that now at length you have revived your concern for me. You were indeed concerned for me, but you had no opportunity. ¹¹ Not that I am speaking of being in need, for I have learned in whatever situation I am to be content. ¹² I know how to be brought low, and I know how to abound. In any and every circumstance, I have learned the secret of facing plenty and hunger, abundance and need. ¹³ I can do all things through him who strengthens me. ¹⁴ Yet it was kind of you to share my trouble. ¹⁵ And you Philippians yourselves know that in the beginning of the gospel, when I left Macedonia, no church entered into partnership with me in giving and receiving, except you only. ¹⁶ Even in Thessalonica you sent me help for my needs once and again. ¹⁷ Not that I seek the gift, but I seek the fruit that increases to your credit. ¹⁸ I have received full payment, and more. I am well supplied, having received from Epaphroditus the gifts you sent, a fragrant offering, a sacrifice acceptable and pleasing to God. ¹⁹ And my God will supply every need of yours according to his riches in glory in Christ Jesus. ²⁰ To our God and Father be glory forever and ever. Amen. [21] Greet every saint in Christ Jesus. The brothers who are with me greet you. [22] All the saints greet you, especially those of Caesar's household. [23] The grace of the Lord Jesus Christ be with your spirit. (Philippians 4:10–23)

WHAT THIS MEANT TO THEM

Paul was supported by the Philippian church from the very beginning through their prayers, their encouragement, and their finances. When he left Philippi and went on to Thessalonica, the Philippian Christians helped him financially. They continued to do so by sending a gift with Epaphroditus, and Paul is acknowledging how much that gift meant to him. He also makes clear that the giving of the gift was just as much a blessing for them as it was for him. In fact, he says, it may be more important for them to give because Paul always had his needs met by the Lord and had learned to be content, no matter his circumstances.

The Philippians were well aware of the kinds of situations Paul had faced—both in suffering and abundance. They witnessed his reaction to his imprisonment and beating in Philippi and knew firsthand that he approached all of life with the same trust in Christ and focus on the gospel, regardless of the situation.

Paul and Silas and the rest of Paul's entourage were well cared for in the first several weeks of spreading the gospel in Philippi. Enjoying the patronage of Lydia, they had a nice home in which to rest, and good meals every day. During that time, their focus was on the mission of the gospel. They were not sidetracked by their comfortable surroundings. When Paul and Silas were arrested and beaten, their focus and demeanor remained the same. Jesus and His gospel was ever their priority, and exchanging a comfortable bed in Lydia's house for the stocks on the floor of the prison did not change that.

MORE BLESSED TO GIVE THAN RECEIVE

In verse 17, Paul said he was not seeking their gift for his account, but for theirs. This is perfectly aligned with what he said in Acts 20:35: that is it more blessed to give than to receive. In Acts, he is quoting something Jesus had said but that the gospel writers hadn't recorded. Because Paul has learned to be content, no matter his situation, he was not really in need of their gift. If they did not give it, God would supply his need in some other way. However, the Philippians needed to give the gift for their own *growth in Christ*.

The reason they needed to make the gift was rooted in verse 18. The gift was "a fragrant offering, a sacrifice acceptable and pleasing to God." This is the language of worship. The aroma would be an allusion to the

> The Philippians needed to give the gift for their own growth in Christ.

burning of incense that rises up in worship. Incense was, at times, seen as representing the prayers of God's people rising up to Him (Psalm 141:2). An acceptable and pleasing sacrifice to God would have been understood as an act of worship in both the Jewish and Greco-Roman cultures of the day. The Philippians knew that their sacrificial giving was not only a benefit to Paul and his ministry, but more importantly, it was an act of worship on their part that demonstrated a love for God and His mission. Paul wrote this as an encouragement to them.

By giving the gift, the Philippians were not left poorer or in desperate need. Paul encourages them that just as God had always supplied whatever he needed, God would also supply all they needed through Christ Jesus. God could supply whatever they needed because His riches are endless. He supplied their need according to His riches in glory. That points to God's overwhelming abundance and ability to meet every need. Not only does it point to God's ability, it also assured them of *His willingness* to supply all that they needed because he did it through Christ Jesus the Lord. Once again, Paul brings the focus back to the gospel of Jesus.

The greatest need they had, the need for a restored relationship with God, was met through Jesus' death, resurrection, and ascension. If God was willing to go to such lengths to meet their most pressing need through Jesus, how much more would He be willing to meet their lesser needs in life through Jesus? The Philippians could rest in the confidence that just as God had supplied Paul's needs, He would surely supply whatever the Philippians needed as well.

THE REACH OF THE GOSPEL

In his farewell, Paul made a statement that had to be incredibly encouraging to the Philippians. It was especially encouraging because of the high number of former Roman soldiers in the city and the fact that Philippi was a Roman colony. Paul sends greetings from all the saints—and especially those of Caesar's household. For this band of

Jesus-followers in the midst of a city highly devoted to the worship of Caesar and loyalty to Caesar, even the idea that some in Caesar's own household had come to faith in Christ was news received with joy and wonder.

Those in Caesar's household may not have been actual blood relatives to Nero since the "household" included anyone who was under the patronage of Caesar: soldiers, counselors, servants, and so on. They were all part of the household of Caesar, just as Lydia's household or the Philippian jailer's household would have included anyone who was under their patronage: blood relatives, servants, even slaves.

By ending his letter with this enormously encouraging greeting, Paul was letting the Philippian Christians know that the gospel was indeed moving forward! Imagine their happiness upon hearing that the kingdom of God was expanding, even into the very heart of the Roman Empire. The common phrase among many Romans in Philippi may have been that Caesar was Lord, but the foundation of that belief was beginning to crack. Even some of those most closely connected to Caesar were coming to new life in Christ.

WHAT IT MEANS TO US

Philippians 4:13 may be one of the most popular verses in the entire Christian world. Athletes keep this reference under their eyes on game days. People often quote it in the face of some challenge. My wife teaches at a Christian school and one year the teachers were asked to list their favorite verse. One out of every three teachers listed Philippians 4:13!

I can do all things through Christ who strengthens me.

I suppose we should not be surprised that teachers lean into this verse a lot or that athletes or people trying to overcome challenges find comfort and strength in these words, but I have a strong suspicion that a vast majority are actually missing the point and context of what Paul is saying.

The focus of Paul's words was that he had learned to be content, no matter his circumstance. He had learned to be content when he was free to go about his mission from one town to the next, sharing the gospel and strengthening the churches. He was also content when he was beaten and under arrest for that very same gospel and mission. He had learned to be content and handle abundance and comfort, and he had learned to be content when he had little and was hungry. Paul listed contrasting situations, making it clear that *his situation didn't matter*. He had learned *through the strength of Jesus Christ* to be content, no matter what.

While it might seem like it made sense that Paul would need the strength of Christ to learn to be content when things were going badly, here's the question: Why would he need that to be content when things were going well? When his belly was full, his purse jingled with coins, his bed was soft, and people were coming to faith in Jesus by the hundreds and happy to hear him? Wouldn't those situations be easy to deal with?

Perhaps these words from Proverbs 30 will help us shed light on what Paul is talking about:

Two things I ask of you; deny them not to me before I die: Remove far from me falsehood and lying; give me neither poverty nor riches;

feed me with the food that is needful for me, lest I be full and deny you and say, "Who is the Lord?" or lest I be poor and steal and profane the name of my God. (Proverbs 30:7-9)

There is a danger in both the lack of resources and the abundance of them. Both can lead to a break in our relationship with the Lord. In one case we can be tempted to acquire things through dishonest means. We may not outright steal things, but we might cut corners, fudge reports, do less than our best for our employer and justify it as not getting paid enough.

Perhaps the greater danger (in our culture anyway) is abundance. We can easily forget the Lord because we have so much. Paul believed he needed Christ's strength in order to be content, even in abundance. I believe there is a strong connection between what he is saying about abundance and what the writer of Proverbs is saying about forgetting the Lord in such times. There is an allure to abundance. The more you have, the more you want. There is always something more that catches our eye. Do we have the latest smartphone? No? You might be missing out! You have a four bedroom two bath house, but you really want that third bathroom (or 5th bedroom). You have a great job, better than you ever thought you would have, but the next promotion looks promising. What do you have to do to get there?

The danger in those times of abundance is twofold. First, it is forgetting to rely on the Lord because we have so much and are not desperate for Him. The second is that we become too focused on what we don't have, and dedicate our lives *to getting* it, because we are not content with what the Lord has done for us. Instead, we begin to push

God out of our lives and run the risk of doing some of the same things the poor do in Proverbs 30:7-9.

While there is nothing inherently wrong with looking to Philippians 4:13 for strength in times of hardship, that is not Paul's main point. His point is learning to trust the Lord, and rest in contentment. Whatever the Lord is doing in your life is enough, according to Paul. If you are striving after things: after fame, after comfort, or anything else that is only of this world, then it will be very difficult to be content in all situations. But if your focus, like that of Paul, is to bring glory to God and find reason to rejoice in all things, then it is possible, through the strength of Christ Jesus, to be content, no matter the circumstance. Why? Because in each and every circumstance, you are looking for what the Lord is doing, what He is teaching you, how you can share and demonstrate the gospel to others who need Jesus. Your focus is on Him, no matter what.

> In each and every circumstance, you are looking for what the Lord is doing.

THE POWER AND DANGER OF CELEBRITY CHRISTIANS

Being told that some in Caesar's household had come to faith in Jesus had to be a great encouragement to the Philippians. Today when we hear of someone who is well known, popular, or powerful comes to

Christ, there is still reason to celebrate. This brings a validation of our faith when someone in the public eye identifies with Christ. That is very natural and not a bad thing.

Yet, it is interesting that Paul does not name anyone in particular. He just makes it known that there are people in Caesar's household who now follow Christ. Maybe it was because of concern for those folks and the sensitive position they were in that he did not use their names. Maybe it was because the Philippians would not have known the names anyway. Or maybe it was because he did not want to put undue pressure and reliance on some other person's fame or position as a support to our faith.

It is not unheard of for some famous person to make a profession of faith in Christ, be immediately thrust in the limelight, held up as a Christian role model, and launched into a speaking circuit—long before they are spiritually mature and ready. Oftentimes, the results are disastrous. They stumble and fall as we all do, but their notoriety makes it seem worse. They have a faith, that while genuine, is uninformed, and they say things that make us cringe. Eventually we move on from them, and might even begin to have doubts about our faith too, all because they didn't turn out so well.

Having role models in the faith is a biblical concept, but just because someone is a celebrity, even a celebrity pastor (the very phrase makes me cringe but it is a common enough phenomenon), that doesn't make them automatically qualified as an example of following Christ. We need to be very careful about placing too much pressure and temptation to be amazing on these folks. We also need to be careful not to place too much of our faith in Christ in the hands of human beings who are broken people, just like we all are.

CONCLUSION

Paul was facing possible execution for his faith in Jesus Christ. Prior to this, he had dealt with beatings, torture, shipwreck, hunger, illness, and more in his efforts to share the gospel and strengthen followers of Jesus and their churches. The Philippians faced suspicion and rejection from the emperor-worshiping Roman citizens in Philippi. Epaphroditus had nearly died during his time serving Paul on behalf of the Philippian church.

Their various situations were not unique among Christians in the first century. After the Day of Pentecost, the apostles were arrested and beaten for their faith. Stephen, one of the original seven deacons of the church in Jerusalem, was stoned to death when he testified of the gospel and the resurrection of Jesus to the people in Jerusalem. Following his martyrdom, a violent persecution broke out against the church, led by a young Pharisee named Saul. Saul was eventually confronted by the risen Jesus, and in the process became Paul, the eventual author of this letter.

In spite of all his suffering, pain, rejection, and hardship, the call to rejoice was the hallmark of his letter. Paul's statement of being able to do all things through Christ who strengthened him (Philippians 4:13), meant he was able to rejoice—no matter what. Such rejoicing does not depend on temporary circumstances, good or bad. It is based rather on the good news of Jesus—that all who trust in Him can enjoy a restored relationship with God because Jesus became a servant to the point of death on a cross. That death was not the end of the story. No, not even close! He rose from the dead! Even the miracle of the resurrection was not the end of the story though. After that, He ascended on high and is seated at the right hand of the Father. The day will come when every knee will bow and every tongue confess that Jesus Christ is Lord to the glory of God the Father (Philippians 2:10-11).

BIBLIOGRAPHY

"Braveheart quote." Quotegeek. May 16, 2012. Accessed August 06, 2019. http://quotegeek.com/quotes-from-movies/braveheart/1150/.

Bruce, F. F. *Understanding the Bible Series Commentary: Philippians.* Grand Rapids, Michigan: Baker Books, 1983.

Calvin, J. *Galatians, Ephesians, Philippians and Colossians.* Edinburgh: Oliver and Boyd, 1965.

Carson, D. A. *Basics for Believers, an Exposition of Philippians.* Grand Rapids Michigan: Baker Academic, 1996.

Cohick, L. H. *The Story of God Bible Commentary: Philippians.* Grand Rapids, Michigan: Zondervan, 2013.

Fee, G. D. *Paul's Letter to the Philippians.* Grand Rapids, Michigan: Eerdmans, 1995.

Lewis, C. S. *God in the Dock: Essays on Theology and Ethics.* Grand Rapids, Michigan: Eerdmans, 1970.

Logos Bible Software 8.6. Mac. Bellingham, Washington: Faithlife Corporation, 2019.

Martin, R. P. *A Hymn of Christ.* Downer's Grove, Illinois: Intervarsity Press, 1997.

Martin, R. P. *Philippians.* London: Oliphants, 1976.

Meilaender, Gilbert. "Friendship in the Classical World." First Things. May 01, 1999. Accessed August 08, 2019. https://www.firstthings.com/article/1999/05/friendship-in-the-classical-world.

O'Brien, P. T. *The Epistle to the Philippians.* Grand Rapids, Michigan: Eerdmans, 1991.

Schnabel, E. *Acts.* Grand Rapids, Michigan: Zondervan, 2012.

Silva, Moisés. *The Wycliffe Exegetical Commentary: Philippians.* Chicago: Moody Press, 1989.

IF YOU'RE A FAN OF THIS BOOK, WILL YOU HELP ME SPREAD THE WORD?

There are several ways you can help me get the word out about the message of this book...

- Post a 5-Star review on Amazon.

- Write about the book on your Facebook, Twitter, Instagram – any social media you regularly use!

- If you blog, consider referencing the book, or publishing an excerpt from the book with a link back to my website. You have my permission to do this as long as you provide proper credit and backlinks.

- Recommend the book to friends – word-of-mouth is still the most effective form of advertising.

- Purchase additional copies to give away as gifts. You can do that by going to my website at: www.danlacich.com

The best way to connect with me is via email at dlacich@gmail.com

If you have not already read it you may also enjoy my other book, *The Provocative God: Radical Things God Has Said and Done*

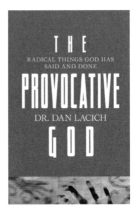

You can order these books from AMAZON & B&N or where ever you purchase your favorite books. You can also order these books from my website at: www.danlacich.com

Need a speaker for your next program?

Invite me to speak to your group or ministry. I have many years of public speaking experience on every continent except Antarctica. If you would like to have me come speak to your group or at an upcoming event, please contact me at: dlacich@gmail.com